DAVID
BERGER

CHRISTIAN
DANCY

MARC
SCHWARTZ

STREAMLINED
Sibelius®

Shortcuts to Professional-looking Music in 3 Easy Lessons

Templates and House Style Included
at www.SuchSweetThunderMusic.com

Such Sweet Thunder

Such Sweet Thunder Publishing
www.SuchSweetThunderMusic.com

STREAMLINED SIBELIUS®

David Berger, Christian Dancy, and Marc Schwartz

Copyright ©2021 by Such Sweet Thunder Publishing

For more information, or if you have questions about this disclaimer, please write to us at: **information@SuchSweetThunderMusic.com.**

Download the online resources for this book at **www.SuchSweetThunderMusic.com**. Fill out the form and you will receive a link to the files.

Book and Cover Design by
Nina Schwartz/Impulse Graphics
ISBN: 978-1-7335931-1-3
First Edition: January 1, 2022
Manufactured in the United States of America

Contents

Preface

There is a revolution going on. It was started centuries ago in Germany by a man named Gutenberg. He invented the printing press, which gave books to the masses, but also started the gradual devaluation of individuality. Why write it out by hand if you could just buy a printed copy? The invention of the typewriter, and then the electric typewriter, set a standard for business (and later, high school term papers). Who wants to wrestle with trying to decipher someone's handwriting when a machine can make it look like a printed book? The computer put the final nail in that coffin. It's amazing to me that schools still teach handwriting.

When I was in elementary school, we all studied penmanship. There were standards of how to shape letters and punctuation. We all did our best to copy the teacher's models off the blackboard. Beauty and grace were admired and rewarded. Over the next few years we all developed our own styles, preferring what looked nice to us, and what came easiest and was fastest to write.

I've always found handwriting styles interesting. So have historians and the police. But in our computer world, the handwriting expert may be going the way of the blacksmith. We have agreed to sacrifice this area of originality for the convenience of ease of reading.

A parallel revolution is happening in the music world. For hundreds of years composers wrote music with pen and ink, first in their scores, and then laboriously extracting the orchestral parts—successful composers and arrangers had their students or paid copyists do this work. Along came music engraving in the 19th century and, by the mid-20th century, only professional musicians read handwritten music. Amateurs played from printed music that was engraved.

It was inevitable with the increasing popularity of computers that music-writing software would follow and proliferate. At first, the programs were slow, awkward and counterintuitive. But then Sibelius® came along and simplified the process, making it accessible even to musicians and amateurs with limited musical knowledge.

Detail, G.F. Handel, The King Shall Rejoice, autograph score. Public domain. Source: The British Library.

This amazing program is so easy to use that many composers and arrangers don't even *own* pencils and score paper—they write directly into the computer. The percentage of composers, arrangers, and orchestrators who still write by hand is minuscule and decreasing daily.

Since Sibelius® is so accessible, most composers, arrangers, and orchestrators turn out the final copies of their scores and parts themselves, thus saving the expense of hiring a copyist. Their music is generally easier to read than if they wrote it by hand. But since few of them have worked as professional copyists, their scores and parts may not be up to industry standards, and can be misleading and difficult for musicians to understand and play at sight.

Having started out in the music business 50 years ago, I came up writing and playing handwritten charts. I was taught how to write scores in pencil and parts in ink. In my 20's

I worked in New York as a trumpet player, arranger, and composer in the jazz and commercial music fields. By the time I was 25, I was busy enough to have my charts copied by Bill Rowen, a professional copyist. Bill had a beautiful hand and laid out his scores and parts in such a way that it was almost impossible to make a mistake when you sight-read them. They looked so artistic and orderly that they made you feel good to read them.

Bill worked in a copying office with about ten other independent copyists, an arranger's room (that I sometimes used), and a printer, who operated a huge Ozalid® copier and taped pages and bound scores. When a big job came, the other copyists would pitch in. I can remember shows I arranged where the whole office would be copying my scores at the same time; Bill supervised them. It was a real factory of craftsmen. Every one of them was a player and had gotten into the copying business

Detail, Paul Dresser, (1897) On the Banks of the Wabash, Far Away. Public domain via Wikimedia.org.

Marlowe - Part I

David Berger,
Score detail,
Marlowe, ©2006.
Created with
Sibelius®.

because it was steady, well-paid work. Every day they churned out jingles, record dates, shows, films, and every other kind of music you can think of. There were a dozen or so similar offices like that in New York. The same was true of Los Angeles and, to a lesser extent, the other cities with a recording industry.

When my own work was slow, Bill would call me from time to time to help him copy a job. It was a learn-while-you-earn situation. He taught me all the rules and conventions, as well as all the little things he had figured out that made his parts so easy to read.

In 1994, when Bill retired, I was doing a lot of work for Jazz at Lincoln Center. They assigned me two excellent copyists: Randa Kirschbaum and Todd Bashore, who copied hundreds of charts for me over many years. Randa used a

program called Score®, and Todd used Finale®. We devised a style sheet that gave our music a professional look.

In this book Marc, Christian, and I will teach you how to create scores and parts with Sibelius® that conform to commercial copying standards and look clean and easy to read. We take into account the players' psychology and reading habits. Since this book is specifically designed for Sibelius® users, we give you all the **templates**, **settings**, and **shortcuts**. Once you start using them, your copying time will be cut in half. Best of all, your musicians will make fewer mistakes, ask fewer questions, and compliment you on how beautiful your parts look.

David Berger
November 2020

Getting Started

This book is designed to teach advanced concepts in Sibelius® in a simple, easy to follow manner. The result will be professional-looking music created to industry standards. We have attempted to make this as surefire and painless as possible. In fact, just by using our Templates (settings, fonts, and preferences), you'll be 90 percent of the way there.

The purpose of written music is to convey the composer's or arranger's intention to the performers in the most expedient way. The system we use in Western music is over 500 years old. Although it has evolved over time, it has remained constant for the last 100 years or so, with the universal proliferation of sheet music. The advantage of conforming to publishing standards is that your music can be easily read by trained musicians.

Sibelius® has most of the rules of standard notation built into it, so it isn't necessary to learn what Sibelius® already knows. But knowledge of the engraving rules can only work to your advantage. This book teaches some of these rules in context. There will always be some points that will need a little tweaking on your end to make your scores and parts more instantly readable. This book will teach you the concepts for making your music look professional, as well as how to use the Sibelius® program to do it. In addition to legibility, we give you tools that drastically reduce the time it takes to "engrave" the music.

We assume that you have gone through the Sibelius® tutorial and have a working knowledge of the basic skills. If not, do that now. The Sibelius® tutorial can be found in **File > Help > Sibelius Tutorials**.

We're going to provide you with two Templates pre-loaded with settings in order for you to get great-looking lead sheets, scores and parts. If you wish to make some alterations or create your own House Style, we suggest that you try our settings first, and get familiar with our reasoning. After that, you will be in a good position to make your own judgments. Bear in mind that our House Style and operation of Sibelius® works well and is aesthetically pleasing to look at. There is no need to make any changes, except to express any aesthetic or functional need specific to your taste and music.*

Visit **www.SuchSweetThunderMusic.com**, fill out the form, and you will receive a link to the Resources for this book. Save the folder to your hard drive.

Installing our Lead Sheet Template

1. Open your Resources folder and double-click the file **Streamlined Sibelius LEAD-SHEET. sib** to open it. Now you are in the Sibelius® program.

2. In the upper left corner of the Sibelius® window, click on **File > Export > Manuscript Paper**.

3. In the **Export Manuscript Paper** menu, type **Streamlined Sibelius LEAD-SHEET** as the name. Make sure that **Keep Title, Composer, etc.** is checked. Under **Category**, check **Other** and name it: **Streamlined Sibelius TEMPLATES**. (See *Figure 0.1*, next page.)

4. Click **Export**.

* We will be releasing custom templates for other size ensembles and instrumentations, such as Pop, Jazz, Chamber, Small Ensemble, Large Ensemble, etc. Visit **www.suchsweetthundermusic.com/collections/ ebooks** and click on *Streamlined Sibelius®* for updated information.

Installing The Plug-ins and Shortcuts

Your version of Sibelius® may or may not have some of these plug-ins and shortcuts, so we are providing a list of how to install each.

They will save you a lot of time when inputting music into your score—and are much easier to remember than having to navigate the program every time. We advise printing out pp. 78–79 and keeping them near your computer as a handy reference.

Plug-ins

• Position Rehearsal Marks

1. From the Ribbon, select **File**, followed by **Plug-ins** at the bottom left, then **Install Plug-ins**.

2. At the top, click on the box next to **Show**, then select **All Plug-ins**.

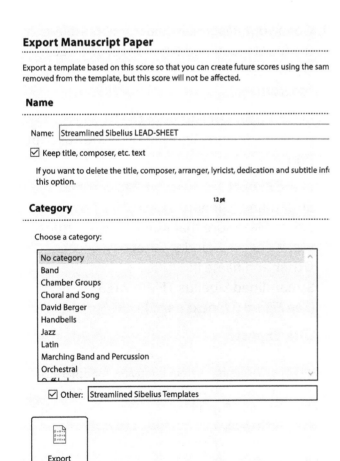

Figure 0.1: Installing the lead sheet template.

3. Scroll down and select **Text**, then scroll down and select **Position Rehearsal Marks**. Then select **Install** at the bottom right of the screen.

4. Press **OK**, then **Close**. This plug-in is now installed.

• Open Selected Parts

1. From the Ribbon, select **File**, followed by **Plug-ins** at the bottom left, then **Install Plug-ins**.

2. At the top, click on the box next to **Show**, then select **All Plug-ins**.

3. Scroll down and select **Other**. Then scroll down and select **Open Selected Parts**. Select **Install** at the bottom right of the screen.

4. Press **OK**, then **Close**. This plug-in is now installed.

Shortcuts

Before installing any shortcuts, we have to install our custom **Feature Set**. This is what Sibelius calls our own shortcuts menu.

1. From the Ribbon, select **File**, then **Preferences**.

2. Select **Keyboard Shortcuts**.

3. In the top middle of the page select **Add Feature Set**.

4. A box will appear. Title your featured set **My Shortcuts** or **Streamlined Sibelius Shortcuts**. Then select **OK**.

5. From here you must once again select **OK**.

• Select All Highlighted Chord Symbols

1. From the Ribbon, select **File**, then **Preferences**.

2. Select **Keyboard Shortcuts**.

3. In the column under **Tab or Category**, select **Home Tab**. Then, under **Feature**, select **Filter Chord Symbols**.

4. Press **Add**.

5. At this screen, press **Alt+K** (⌥A).
   Then press **OK**.

6. Press **OK** at the bottom of the screen.
   This shortcut is now installed.

• Select All Highlighted Lyrics

1. From the Ribbon, select **File**, then **Preferences**.

2. Select **Keyboard Shortcuts**.

3. In the column under **Tab or Category** select **Home Tab.** Then, under **Feature**, select **Filter Lyrics**.

4. Press **Add**.

5. At this screen, press **Alt+L** (⌥L).
   Then press **OK**.

6. Press **OK** at the bottom of the screen.
   This shortcut is now installed.

• Open Edit Text Styles Menu

1. From the Ribbon, select **File**, then **Preferences**.

2. Select **Keyboard Shortcuts**.

3. In the column under **Tab or Category**, select **Text Tab**. Then under **Feature**, select **Edit Text Styles**.

4. Press **Add**.

5. At this screen, press **Ctrl+Shift+Alt+T** (⌘⇧⌥T). Then press **OK**.

6. Press **OK** at the bottom of the screen.
   This shortcut is now installed.

• Go Back to Keypad Panel 1

1. From the Ribbon, select **File**, then **Preferences**.

2. Select **Keyboard Shortcuts**.

3. In the column under **Tab or Category** select **Keypad (all).** Under **Feature,** for PC: Type **Shift and +** on the numpad (numeric keyboard on the right side of your keyboard). For Mac, select **−** on the keypad.

4. Press **Add**.

5. At this screen, press **Shift** and the **+** sign on the **numpad**. Then press **OK**.

6. Press **OK** at the bottom of the screen.
   This shortcut is now installed.

• Show Information in Score, But Not in Parts

1. From the Ribbon, select **File**, then **Preferences**.

2. Select **Keyboard Shortcuts**.

3. In the column under **Tab or Category** select **Home Tab**. Then under **Feature**, select **Show in Score**.

4. Press **Add**.

5. At this screen, press **Ctrl+[** (⌘[).
   Then press **OK**.

6. Press **OK** at the bottom of the screen.
   This shortcut is now installed.

• Show Information in Parts, But Not in Score

1. From the Ribbon, select **File**, then **Preferences**.

2. Select **Keyboard Shortcuts**.

3. In the column under **Tab or Category** select **Home Tab.** Then, under **Feature**, select **Show in Parts**.

4. Press **Add**.

5. At this screen, press **Ctrl+]** (⌘]).
   Then press **OK**.

6. Press **OK** at the bottom of the screen.
   This shortcut is now installed.

• Make Selected Measures Into a Page

1. From the Ribbon, select **File**, then **Preferences**.

2. Select **Keyboard Shortcuts**.

3. In the column under **Tab or Category** select **Layout tab**. Then select **Make Into Page**.

4. Press **Add**.

5. At this screen, press **Ctrl+Shift+Alt+M** (⌘⇧⌥M). Then press **OK**.

6. Press **OK** at the bottom of the screen. This shortcut is now installed.

• Create a Repeat Bar

1. From the Ribbon, select **File**, then **Preferences**.

2. Select **Keyboard Shortcuts**.

3. In the column under **Tab or Category** select **Keypad (jazz articulations)**. Then under **Feature**, select **Repeat Bar**.

4. Press **Add**.

5. At this screen press **Ctrl+Alt+5** (⌘⌥5). Then press OK.

6. Press **OK** at the bottom of the screen. This shortcut is now installed.

• Open Position Rehearsal Marks

1. From the Ribbon, select **File**, then **Preferences**.

2. Select **Keyboard Shortcuts**.

3. In the column under **Tab or Category** select **Plug-ins**. Under **Feature**, select **Position Rehearsal Marks**.

4. Press **Add**.

5. At this screen, press **Ctrl+Alt+P** (⌘⌥P). Then press **OK**.

6. Press **OK** at the bottom of the screen. This shortcut is now installed.

• Turn Note into a Grace Note

1. From the Ribbon, select **File**, then **Preferences**.

2. Select **Keyboard Shortcuts**.

3. In the column under **Tab or Category** select **Note Input Tab**. Under **Feature**, select **Turn note into grace note**.

4. Press **Add**.

5. At this screen press **;** then press **OK**.

6. Press **OK** at the bottom of the screen. This shortcut is now installed.

• Optimize Staff Spacing

1. From the Ribbon, select **File**, then **Preferences**.

2. Select **Keyboard Shortcuts**.

3. In the column under **Tab or Category**, select **Layout tab** followed by **Optimize Staff Spacing**.

4. Press **Add**.

5. At this screen press **Ctrl+Alt+S** (⌘⌥S. Then press **OK**.

6. Press **OK** at the bottom of the screen. This shortcut is now installed.

• Split System/Measures or Indent Coda

1. From the Ribbon, select **File**, then **Preferences**.

2. Select **Keyboard Shortcuts**.

3. In the column under **Tab or Category**, select **Layout Tab**. Under **Feature**, select **Split System**.

4. Press **Add**.

5. At this screen, press **Alt+S** (⌥S). Then press OK.

6. Press **OK** at the bottom of the screen. This shortcut is now installed.

• Open Selected Parts

1. From the Ribbon, select **File**, then **Preferences**.

2. Select **Keyboard Shortcuts**.

3. In the column under **Tab or Category**, select **Plug-ins**. Under **Feature**, select **Open Selected Parts**.

4. Press **Add**.

5. At this screen press **Ctrl**+**Shift**+**Alt**+**O** (⌘⇧⌥**O**). Then press **OK**.

6. Press **OK** at the bottom of the screen. This shortcut is now installed.

• Copy Part Layout Menu

1. From the Ribbon, select **File**, then **Preferences**.

2. Select **Keyboard Shortcuts**.

3. In the column under **Tab or Category**, select **Parts tab**. Under **Feature**, select **Copy Part Layout**.

4. Press **Add**.

5. At this screen, press **'** (apostrophe). Then press **OK**.

6. Press **OK** at the bottom of the screen. This shortcut is now installed.

Lesson 1. Creating a Lead Sheet

In this lesson, we will take you through the steps to creating a professional lead sheet for the song *Look For The Silver Lining*. Lead sheets are the standard form for notating songs. They contain the melody, chord symbols and lyrics, written on one music staff in the treble clef. The melody goes in the staff; the chord symbols above the staff, and the lyrics below the staff.

What *Not* to Put in a Lead Sheet

- Dynamics
- Articulations
- Rehearsal Letters and Bar Numbers.

Lead sheets are meant to be generic. They are not arrangements. Even putting in a tempo or style can be optional.

Printing Out the Lead Sheet

In the Resources folder, open **Streamlined-Sibelius_Charts.pdf**. Print *Look For The Silver Lining* (first page). You can view this lead sheet on your screen, but printing it out will make it easier to copy.

Creating A New Score

1. Open Sibelius®. This will open the **Quick Start** menu. In the **New Score** tab, scroll down to the category: **Streamlined Sibelius TEMPLATES** and click on **Streamlined Sibelius LEAD-SHEET**. If another score is already open, create a new score by going to **File > New**.

2. In the next menu, select your time signature from **Time Signature Setup**.

3. This song doesn't need a pick-up bar. But when you want to create one, under where it says **Pick-up (Upbeat) Bar**, click on the box,

then enter the appropriate rhythms to fill the pick-up bar.

4. Under where it says **Key Signature Setup**, select the key (**C** for this song).

5. Click on **Create** in the lower right corner of the screen.

6. At this point, you should save your work. Use the shortcut **Ctrl+S** for PC (⌘**S** for Mac) to bring up the **Save** menu.

7. Create a new name for the file and select the folder destination where you want it to be saved on your hard drive. For example, this is how we label our files:

   Filename: **Look For The Silver Lining LEAD-SHEET.sib**
   Folder destination: **My Documents > Sibelius Files > Lead Sheets**

   Save by clicking **Ctrl+S** (⌘**S**).

   NOTE: To be safe, save your work often!

Inputting Full Score Info

Set up Score Info:

1. **File > Info**.

2. **Show Info for:** Select **Full Score** on the drop-down menu.

3. Input:
   Title: **LOOK FOR THE SILVER LINING** (case sensitive)
   Composer: **Music by Jerome Kern**
   Lyricist: **Lyrics by Buddy DeSylva**
   Publisher: **Look For The Silver Lining**
   Copyright: **©2018 Such Sweet Thunder\n\ All Rights Reserved**

   NOTE: To create the copyright symbol © on a PC, hold down **Alt** and press in succession the characters 0169. (Mac: Press ⌥**G**). \n\ is Sibelius® code for "new line."

Show info for: FULL SCORE ∨

Some of the text below may be used in text in your score or parts. For example, Part Name
top of the first and subsequent pages of your parts.

Title:	Part name:
LOOK FOR THE SILVER LINING	FULL SCORE

Subtitle:	Dedication:
	Full Score

Composer:	Lyricist:
Music by Jerome Kern	Lyrics by Buddy DeSylva

Arranger:	Copyist:

Artist:	Publisher:
	Look For The Silver Lining

Instrument changes:

Copyright:

©2018 Such Sweet Thunder\n\All Rights Reserved

Figure 1.1: Inputting full score info.

Setting Up the Page

1. Return to the **Home** tab.

   You will notice that the title looks too big for the page. Our standard font size for titles is 36 point. For long titles, it needs to be smaller to to fit in the page margins.

2. To change the font size, single-click on the title of the song (make sure it is highlighted purple).

3. Press **Ctrl**+**Shift**+**Alt**+**T** (⌘⇧⌥T) to open the **Edit Text Styles** menu.

4. Click **Edit**.

5. Change **Size in Score (Absolute)** to 32 points by typing **32** in the box.

6. Change **Size in Part (Absolute)** to 32 points by typing **32** in the box.

7. Click **OK** to accept the change. (The title should still be highlighted.)

8. Click **Close** to close the **Edit Text Styles** menu.

9. Sibelius® gives you 8 bars to start with. This lead sheet is 32 bars long. To add the other 24 bars, click in bar **8**. Press **Alt**+**B** (⌥B) to

open the **Create Bars** menu. Type **24** in the space provided, and press **Enter (Return)**. Sibelius® will add the desired number of bars after the currently selected bar.

We use double barlines to mark the form of a song. *Look For The Silver Lining* follows the popular 32-bar *abac* song form. There should be a double barline at the end of every 8 measures. This helps performers to understand the form and keep their place.

10. **Right-click** (**^click** for Mac) an open space on the page to open the **Barline** menu.

11. Select **Barline > Double**.

12. Click the barline at the end of bar **8**. Repeat this in bars **16** and **24**.

13. You can also copy and paste barlines. Click on the barline in bar **8**. Press **Ctrl**+**C** (⌘C), click in bar **16**, and press **Ctrl**+**V** (⌘V). Repeat for bar **24**.

    Your score should now look like *Figure 1.2*.

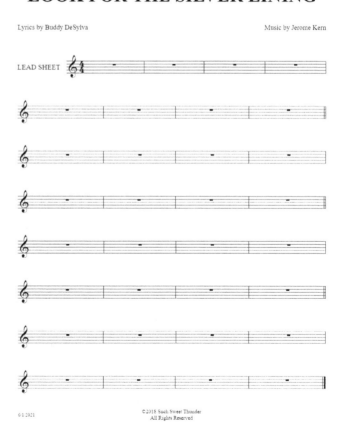

Figure 1.2: Setting up a lead sheet.

Figure 1.3: The Sibelius® Keypad Panel.

Inputting Notes

When you create lead sheets, you need to input three things: **notes**, **chords**, and **lyrics**. Always do them in this order—since in Sibelius®, chord symbols and lyrics are usually attached to specific notes.

The fastest way to input notes is by using the **Sibelius® keypad** *(Figure 1.3)*. If the **Keypad Panel** is not visible, select **View > Panels > Keypad**—or use the shortcut **Ctrl+Alt+K (⌘⌥K)**.*

The keypad is controlled by your computer's keyboard—mainly by the numerical keypad (numpad) on the right-hand side of your keyboard.

If your computer doesn't have a right-hand numerical keypad, it's a good idea to buy an inexpensive Bluetooth or USB keypad to connect while using Sibelius®. Graphics tablets can also be used.

NOTE: Some Sibelius® users prefer to input pitches using external MIDI keyboards. There are pluses and minuses to this method:

* If **Kindle**® is installed on your computer, **Ctrl**+**Alt**+**K** (⌘⌥**K**) may open it. If so, you can toggle the Sibelius® keypad on and off using **View > Panels > Keypad**.

Pluses:
  • Fewer octave adjustments
  • Easier to enter chords.

Minuses:
  • Extra gear to purchase and transport
  • Gear takes up extra space
  • Time consuming to set up and break down
  • Less control of enharmonic spelling.

For information on using a MIDI keyboard to input notes, see the **Sibelius® Reference Guide** section **Input Devices**. Another app you can use to input notes is **Notation Express** with its **Stream Deck Console**. For information, contact www.nycmusicservices.com.

We have found inputting with the keyboard and numpad to be the most efficient method. With practice, inputting pitches with letters on the computer's keyboard becomes automatic.

Notes and Rests

To input the first bar of *Look For The Silver Lining*, you will be typing pitches using your keyboard's letters, A to G; rhythmic values and symbols using the numpad, and **Enter** when you add ties.

1. Click on the **whole rest** in the first bar (make sure the **rest** is highlighted in blue, and not the bar).

2. With the whole rest selected, press **5** on the numpad (to create a half note), and type **E**.

   This creates the half-note **E**, but in the wrong octave. (Sibelius® will pick an octave within a 4th of the previous note.)

   Use the keyboard's arrow keys to move notes up or down. You can either move the **E** down seven steps, or use the shortcut **Ctrl+↓** (⌘↓). This will move the note down a full octave. [Use **Ctrl**+↑ (⌘↑) to move notes up an octave].

   NOTE: Mistakes will happen! Use Undo, **Ctrl**+**Z** (⌘**Z**). In Sibelius®, Undo will take you back one step. Repeat it until you get back

FULL SCORE

LOOK FOR THE SILVER LINING

Lyrics by Buddy DeSylva

Music by Jerome Kern

Figure 1.4: Inputting notes.

to where you need to be. After Undoing, it is always a good idea to **Deselect (ESC)**. Deselect often. When in doubt, Deselect!

3. Now add another half-note **E** with a tie. Press **E**, then **Enter** to add the tie. Sibelius® remembers the last note length you used, so you don't have to select it again.

Fixing Note Errors

If you make a mistake on a pitch, use the ↑ or ↓ arrow to change it. If you have already gone past a note and want to get back to it, press **ESC** and click on the note, using the ↑ or ↓ arrow.

You can also toggle through the notes and rests by using the ← and → arrow keys.

4. **Bar 2:** Press: **4** on the numpad (quarter note) and type: **E, F, D, E.**

This is where the keyboard shines! You are basically typing notes into the score, just as if you were typing text. Once you get comfortable with this process, and the few shortcuts needed, inputting notes will be a breeze. Finish inputting this line.

5. **Bars 3-4:** Now type: **5, C, C, Enter, 4, C, D, E, F.**

   Your result should look like the first 4 bars in *Figure 1.4*.

Rests

6. Continue inputting notes until the last two notes of **bar 6**. Press: **3** to create an eighth note, then type: **A, G, Enter.** Continue through the end of **Bar 7**.

   On the downbeat of **bar 8**, we have our first rest. Type: **4** (quarter note) and **0** (rest). As with notes, always select the rhythm first, and the rest (**0**) after. Continue inputting until **bar 15**.

Dotted Notes

7. The quarter note on the downbeat of **bar 15** has a dot after it.

   Type: **4**, then the dot (.) on the numpad, and finally the letter **G**. Continue inputting notes through **bar 16**.

Copy and Paste

8. Notice that **bars 17–21** are identical to **bars 1–5**. This is a perfect opportunity to use copy and paste.

   Click on an empty space in **bar 1**, so that the entire bar is highlighted blue. Hold down **Shift** and click on an empty space in **bar 5**. This will highlight all 5 bars in blue.

   Press: **Ctrl+C (⌘C)** to copy those bars.

Click on an empty space in **bar 17**, so the entire bar is highlighted blue. Press: **Ctrl+V** (**⌘V**) to paste. This will paste **bars 1–5** into **bars 17–21**.

Keep inputting through the end of **bar 23**.

NOTE: It's always a good idea to copy and paste notes from earlier bars. Even when there are a few changes, it's faster to change a few copied notes than to type every note, one by one.

Accidentals

9. In **bar 24** we have an accidental (**G♯**). To input a **sharp** (♯), press **8** on the numpad before selecting the quarter note (**4** on the numpad). Then, press **G** to create the note.

   Naturals (♮) are **7** on the numpad.
   Flats (♭) are **9** on the numpad.

The Sibelius® keypad has six menus of notes, accidentals and other musical signs. To see the other menus, click on the appropriate icon at the top of the keypad.

To move from one menu to the next, press **+** on the numpad to move forward. To go back to the first menu, either click the first icon, or press **Shift** and press **+** on the numpad. (For Mac, press only the minus sign on the numpad: **–** , not Shift). Another option is to use keys F7–F12, which correspond to the 6 keypad panels.

To change a pre-existing accidental, click on the note and select the desired accidental on your numpad. To cancel an accidental, select the same accidental, and it will disappear.

Complete inputting the remaining notes and rests for the entire song.

Exercise:

Start a new score. Without looking at the directions, try inputting the entire 32 bars—notes and rests only—from the completed lead sheet, using only your keyboard and numpad. You will notice a big increase in your note inputting speed.

Figure 1.5: Inputting notes.

After you finish inputting the notes, your score should look like *Figure 1.5*.

Inputting Chord Symbols

Sibelius® offers several commonly used chord symbols. We have found the publishing standard to be the clearest and the most space-saving. It has been the standard in commercial music and publishing for decades. Here are a few general rules:

Standard Chord Symbols	
Commonly Used	**Publishing Standard**
$C^{7(\flat 9)}$	C^{7-9}
$C\sharp^{7(\sharp 11)}$	$C\sharp^{7+11}$
$C^{-7(\flat 5)}$ or $C^{\varnothing}$	Cm^{7-5}
$C\triangle$	$Cmaj^{7}$
$Cdim^{7}$ or $C^{\circ 7}$	C°

- Avoid parentheses. They are unnecessary, distracting, and take up extra space.

- Flat (♭) and sharp (♯) signs are reserved for the name of the root chord. **+** and **–** signs are used for alterations.

- We use lower case **m** for minor, rather than **–**, to avoid confusion with alterations.

- We use **maj7** for major 7th chords, rather than the delta symbol (△), which in small print can look like the diminished symbol (○).

- All diminished chords include a diminished 7th, so ○ should suffice; no need to write ○7.

- We use **m7-5** rather than the half diminished symbol (∅) to avoid confusion with the diminished symbol (○).

Although we strongly recommend using the publishing standard for chord symbols, we recognize that many musicians have other preferences. If you would like to alter our symbols to your own system: In the **Ribbon**, select **Appearance > Engraving Rules > Chord Symbols**, and make the necessary changes.

Sibelius® makes it easy to input chord symbols. You just type each chord as if you were saying it. For example, to type C7+9, you just type: C, 7, +, 9.

1. Select the first note (**E**) and type the shortcut **Ctrl+K (⌘K)** to **Create Chord Symbol Text**.

2. Type your first chord symbol: **C**. Chord symbols are case sensitive; we use UPPER CASE for the root, and lower case for the chord quality (ex. **Cmaj7**). But you don't have to capitalize while typing in chord symbols; Sibelius® will make the necessary corrections for you.

3. Press the **space bar** twice, to move to the chord on beat **3**.

   In a bar with only quarter note or longer values, the space bar lets you put chords over the downbeats of the bar. This is the most common place for chord changes to occur. When there is a rhythm shorter than a quarter note, Sibelius® will let you put a chord symbol on each note.

   Press **Tab** to skip to the beginning of the next bar.

4. For the second chord (**Am7**), type: A, m, 7. With the help of our pre-settings, Sibelius® will automatically format the **7** as a superscript **7**.

5. Input the chord symbols for the first 9 bars.

The chords for *Look For The Silver Lining* are quite simple, so we will skip to three common chord changes that you need to know how to type, in order of their appearance. After you type each chord, input the chords up to the next example.

6. **Bar 10** has a **G7/F**. Slash chords are just as easy as they look. Type: **G, 7, /, F**.

7. **Bar 14** has an **F♯m7-5**. When there is a sharp in the root chord, we type the **number** or **pound** symbol (♯). This chord should be input as: **F, #, m, 7, –, 5**.

   For **flats**, use the letter **b**. Sibelius® will convert it to a flat sign (♭).

8. **Bar 26** has a **D♯○**. Diminished symbols are most easily input by typing the lower case letter **o**. Again, Sibelius® will change it to a diminished symbol (○).

Copying and Pasting Chord Symbols

The chords for **bars 17–20** are identical to those for **bars 1–4**. In order to copy the chord changes:

1. Select **bars 1–4**.

2. Press shortcut **Alt+K (⌥K)**. This will select only the chord symbols.

3. Copy: **Ctrl+C (⌘C)**.

4. Select **bar 17**.

5. Paste: **Ctrl+V (⌘V)**.

LOOK FOR THE SILVER LINING

Lyrics by Buddy DeSylva   Music by Jerome Kern

Figure 1.6: Inputting chord symbols.

6. Finish inputting the rest of the chords. You should end up with a lead sheet that looks like *Figure 1.6*.

Inputting Lyrics

With lyrics, as with notes and chords, Sibelius® does much of the work for you. There are publishing standards for how lyrics should look on the page, and the program does a great job of providing most of these.

There are only a few extra things you need to know. Like chord symbols, lyrics attach to certain notes in the bar, just as they do in performance of the music.

1. Select the first note (**E**) and type the shortcut **Ctrl+L (⌘L)** to **Create lyric text**.

2. Type your first word: **Look**

   NOTE: Sibelius® does not automatically capitalize words. To capitalize, hold down the **Shift** key and type the letter.

3. In **Lyric text** mode, press the **space bar** to get to the next note. When you input chords, the space bar brings you to the next beat, but in **Lyric text**, it brings you to the next *note* (since a singer would not be singing new words where there are rests).

   Press the **space bar** to move the cursor to the next note (in this case, the **E** on beat **3**). Type the second word: **for**

4. Now press the **space bar**.

   You will notice that Sibelius® doesn't recognize the tie. Instead, it gives you the option to create a lyric under the **E** on beat **1** of **bar 2**.

   There is no lyric here, so press the **space bar** one more time. Sibelius® will automatically create a long line (_____) after the word "**for**," up until beat **1** of **bar 2**. This is common practice for notes that are tied.

5. Let's move forward to the word "**sil-ver**" in **bar 2**. With words of more than one syllable, we use a hyphen (**-**) to connect the syllables. Don't press the space bar.

6. Click the note **D** on beat **3** of **bar 2**. Press **Ctrl+L (⌘L)**.

7. Type: **sil, -, ver**. Press the **space bar** to get to the next word.

This is all the information you need to enter the lyrics for *Look For The Silver Lining*. Input the rest of the lyrics.

When you are finished, you should have a lead sheet that looks like *Figure 1.7*.

NOTE: When there are multiple notes for one syllable, place a slur from the first to the last note. See **Slurs and Phrase Markings**, p. 37.)

LOOK FOR THE SILVER LINING

Lyrics by Buddy DeSylva

Music by Jerome Kern

Figure 1.7: Inputting lyrics, lead sheet view.

Final Steps

Lowering Chord Symbols

To clean up the score a bit, you may need to move the chord symbols down towards the staff, to keep them from bumping into lyrics from the line above.

1. To select All, press **Ctrl+A** (⌘**A**).

2. Press **Alt+K** (⌥**K**) to select (Sibelius® uses the word "filter") *only* the chord symbols.

   NOTE: See the *Sibelius Reference Guide* for information about using the filtering function.

3. Use the ↓ arrow on the keyboard to lower all the chord symbols together. Five clicks is generally enough, depending on how much you are zoomed although it may vary from lead sheet to lead sheet.

Parts View

The product you have at this moment is the **Full Score view**—not what you will be printing out. The full score view is where you input the information, but you will be printing out your lead sheet as a **Part**.

1. Click the **+ button** on the top right of the Sibelius® workspace to see the **Parts** drop-down menu.

2. In the drop-down menu, select the part: **LEAD SHEET**.

Auto-formatting Tools

Sibelius® has two extremely helpful auto-format-ting tools—**Reset Note Spacing** and **Optimize Staff Spacing**—to help you clean up a score before printing it.

As you input, Sibelius® automatically adjusts the spacing between notes. This can occasionally create some awkward spaces, or put acciden-tals too close to the noteheads. **Reset Note Spacing** resets the spacing back to its original setting.

Figure 1.8a: Chord symbols are too high.

Figure 1.8b: Chord symbols are lowered.

Optimize Staff Spacing automatically adjusts the staff placement to give you the clearest spacing possible. Use it to fix awkward spacing of staves, dynamics, and text.

Applying Reset Note Spacing and Optimize Staff Spacing

These two functions will only affect the music within a Selection. Although they usually give good results, it's still possible that something unwanted can occur—be ready to **Undo** if nec-essary.

1. In the **View** tab, select the **Zoom** drop-down menu, and select **Fit Page**. In newer versions of Sibelius®, press shortcut **Ctrl+0** (⌘**0**).

2. Press **Ctrl+A** (⌘**A**) to select everything.

Figure 1.9a: Notes need to be re-spaced.

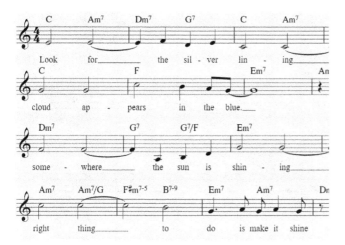

Figure 1.9b: Note spacing is corrected.

3. Press **Ctrl+Shift+N** (⌘⇧**N**) to **Reset Note Spacing**.

4. With your selection still highlighted, press **Ctrl+Alt+S** (⌘⌥**S**) to **Optimize Staff Spacing**.

NOTE: Versions from 2020.1 and later have an **Auto Optimize** feature that you can choose to keep on or off.

In the **Ribbon**, select **Layout**. Under the word **Optimize**, click on **Auto** to toggle it on or off. If it appears in yellow, it is ON.

As with any automatic function (such as Auto-Correct for text), it may not always give the results you want. Further adjustment may be needed.

Before you print, check carefully to make sure there are no accidental collisions. Proofreading your score by eye is always recommended. Give the part a once-over, and if there are no errors, you are good to go. Now your lead sheet is ready to print!

Printing and Exporting to PDF

You will either want to print this lead sheet straight from Sibelius®, or export it to a PDF file to send and/or store on your computer.

To Print from Sibelius®

1. Press **Ctrl+P** (⌘**P**).

2. Make sure that only **Print Parts** is checked.

3. Select the part **LEAD SHEET** from the **Parts** menu.

4. Select your printer.

5. Click **Print**.

To Export to PDF

1. Select the **File** tab; go to **Export**.

Sibelius® offers a vast array of exporting options. To learn more about each, see the *Sibelius® Reference Guide*.

2. Select **PDF** and in the menu, pick **Selection of parts (one file)**.

3. Select **LEAD SHEET** from the **Parts to Export** list.

4. Create a name for the file and select the folder destination on your hard drive.

   For example, this is how we label our files: Filename: **Look For The Silver Lining LEAD SHEET.pdf** Folder destination: **My Documents > PDF Music > Lead Sheets**

5. Click **Export**.

(continued p. 22)

6/1/2021

Figure 1.10: Lead sheet view. Part is ready for printing.

LOOK FOR THE SILVER LINING

Lyrics by Buddy DeSylva

Music by Jerome Kern

Figure 1.11: Lead sheet exported to pdf.

Transposing Lead Sheets

You may need to transpose lead sheets to other keys. This could be for different instruments or to accommodate singers.

To Transpose a Lead Sheet for B♭ Instruments:

1. Press **ESC** to deselect.

2. Press **Shift**+**T** (⇧**T**).

3. Select **Transpose by Key** and select **D**.

4. Whether you transpose up or down depends on the range of the melody. Use your best judgment, according to the range of the instrument or singer. For our purposes, we will select **Closest**.

5. Press either **Enter** or select **OK** on the page. It will automatically transpose everything for you.

NOTE: After transposing, always check for accidentals, and make sure there are no double flats or double sharps. Correct any errors (see **Accidentals**, p. 14).

To Create a Lead Sheet for Bass Clef Instruments:

1. Press **ESC** to deselect.

2. Press shortcut **Q** to select a **Change of Clef**.

3. Select **bass clef**. Click on the treble clef to paste the bass clef in its place.

4. The chart will now be written in the same octave, but in bass clef.

5. Press **Ctrl**+**A** (⌘**A**) again to select everything.

6. Press **Ctrl**+↓ (⌘↓) to transpose all notes down an octave.

Figure 1.12: Lead sheet view, transposed for B♭ instruments.

Lesson 1 Shortcuts Quick Reference			
Ctrl+↓ (⌘↓)	Move note/s **down 1 octave.**	**Ctrl+Shift+Alt+T** (⌘⇧⌥T)	Open **Edit Text Styles** menu.*
Ctrl+↑ (⌘↑)	Move note/s **up one octave.**	**Crtl+Alt+K** (⌘⌥K)	Open **Keypad** Panel.
Alt+B (⌥B)	Open **Create Bars** menu.	**Ctrl+0** (⌘0)	**Fit page** on screen.
Ctrl+S (⌘S)	**Save File.**	**+** on numpad	Go to **next Keypad Panel.**
Ctrl+Z (⌘Z)	**Undo**—Go back 1 step.	**Shift** and **+** on numpad (Mac: **−** symbol only, no Shift)	Go back to **first Keypad Panel.***
Ctrl+K (⌘K)	Create **Chord Symbol** text.		
Alt+K (⌥A)	Select **all highlighted chord symbols.***		
Ctrl+L (⌘L)	Create **Lyric** text.	**Ctrl+P** (⌘P)	Open **Print menu.**
Alt+L (⌥L)	Select **all highlighted lyrics.***	**Shift+T** (⇧T)	Open **Transpose menu.**
Ctrl+A (⌘A)	Select **everything.**	**Q**	Open **Change of Clef menu.**
Ctrl+C (⌘C)	**Copy** selected information.	**Ctrl+V** (⌘V)	**Paste.**

* Not standard with Sibelius®. To install, see pp. 6–9.

Figure 1.13: Lead sheet view, transposed for bass clef instruments.

Lesson 2. Creating a Small Group Score

In this chapter, you will learn how to input a full score in Sibelius®. We'll be using a jazz octet arrangement of *In A Persian Market*. The style and instrumentation aren't important; we are just using this score to go through the engraving process in detail. The same procedures apply for virtually all score engraving.

There is a lot of information in this book, and it may take a few repetitions for you to internalize a process. Don't worry—if you forget a procedure, you can look up the shortcut for it in **Shortcuts**, pp. 78–79. If you are still unclear, look up the original explanation. Everyone has their own learning curve. Be patient. Sibelius® is quite intuitive for a program of this complexity. You'll be amazed at how quickly you become proficient.

Printing Our Model Octet Score

In the Resources folder, open **Streamlined-Sibelius_Charts.zip**. Save the folder to your hard drive, open it, and select **In A Persian Market**. Print a hard copy of the full score (pages 2–11 of the pdf) to refer to while you complete this lesson.

Installing Our Octet Template

1. Open your Resources folder and double-click the file name **Streamlined Sibelius OCTET.sib** to open it. Now you are in the Sibelius® program.

2. In the upper left corner of the Sibelius® window, select **File > Export > Manuscript Paper**.

3. In the **Export Manuscript Paper** menu, input: **Streamlined Sibelius OCTET** as the name. Make sure **Keep title, composer, etc.** text is checked. Under **Category**, select Streamlined Sibelius.

4. Click **Export**.

Creating A New Score

1. Create a new score by selecting **File > New**. This will open the **Quick Start** menu.

   In the **New Score** tab, scroll down to the category: **Streamlined Sibelius TEMPLATES** and **single**-click on **Streamlined Sibelius OCTET**.

2. In the next menu, under **Time Signature Setup**, select **5/4**.

3. There is no pickup bar, so move on to **Key Signature**.

4. Under where it says **Key Signature Setup**, select the key of **A minor**. Press **Create**. Save: **Ctrl+S (⌘S)**.

5. Create a new name for the file, and select the folder where you would like it to go on your hard drive. For example, this is how we name and save our files:

   Filename: **In A Persian Market OCTET.sib**
   Folder destination: **My Documents > Sibelius Files > Octets > In A Persian Market**

6. Click **Save**.

Input Full Score Info

Setup Score Info:

1. On the Ribbon, select **File > Info**.

2. Input:
   Title: **IN A PERSIAN MARKET**
   (Type this in ALL CAPS.)
   Composer: **Albert Ketelbey**

Arranger: **arranged by David Berger**
Publisher: **In A Persian Market**
Copyright: **©2015 Such Sweet Thunder\n\ All Rights Reserved**

(For original compositions, no text is needed in the **Arranger** field.)

The copyright symbol © is provided in the template, but if you need to create it: Hold down **Alt**, and type **0169** on the numpad (Mac: Type ⌘**G**).

Input Instrument Information

1. Select **File > Info**.

You'll notice that there are a number of fields that we don't normally use. In our template, we have assigned pertinent information to these fields.

Dedication: We use this field for **Instrument Name**, (use Initial Caps), for parts pages 2 and up.

Publisher: We use this field for the **Title** (use Initial Caps), for score and parts pages 2 and up.

2. Using the table below, for each part, insert the **Part Name**, **Dedication (Instrument Name)**, and **Instrument Changes**.
This information from the Full Score will carry over into the parts.

3. Click the **Home** tab to return to the score view.

A few notes about these settings:

- These inputs are **case-sensitive**. This is **exactly** how they should be typed in, in order to be correct on the score.

- In the **Instrument changes** column, notice the use of the wildcard **\n**. This is Sibelius® code for **new line**. The next instrument will appear under the previous one in the musician's part.

- Notice in the instrument changes column for the three reed parts, we put the instruments in the order in which they are played. This ensures that the reed players are prepared with the correct instruments before the arrangement even starts.

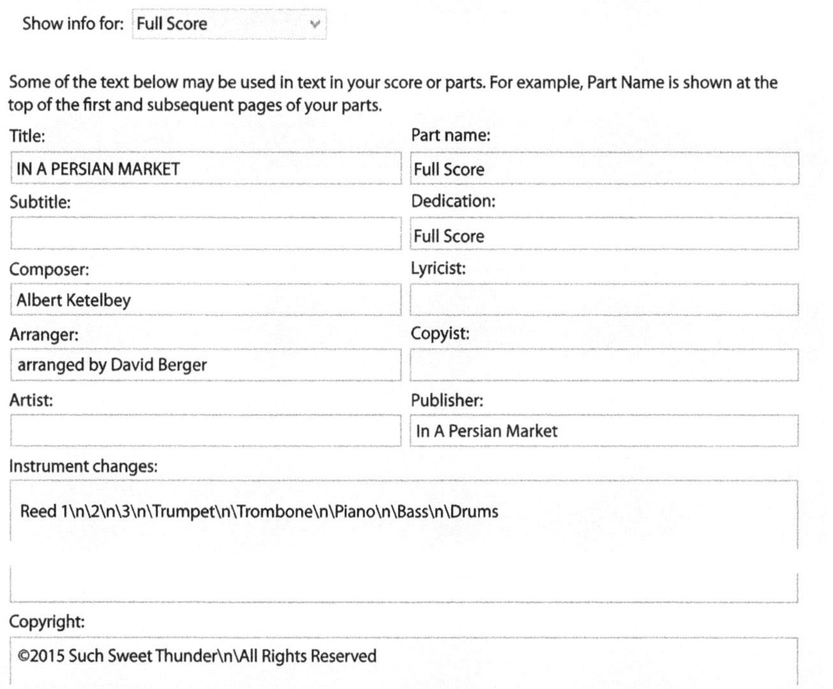

Show info for: Full Score

Some of the text below may be used in text in your score or parts. For example, Part Name is shown at the top of the first and subsequent pages of your parts.

Title:
IN A PERSIAN MARKET

Part name:
Full Score

Subtitle:

Dedication:
Full Score

Composer:
Albert Ketelbey

Lyricist:

Arranger:
arranged by David Berger

Copyist:

Artist:

Publisher:
In A Persian Market

Instrument changes:
Reed 1\n\2\n\3\n\Trumpet\n\Trombone\n\Piano\n\Bass\n\Drums

Copyright:
©2015 Such Sweet Thunder\n\All Rights Reserved

Figure 2.1: Inputting info for the Full Score.

Part Name	Dedication	Instrument changes
REED 1	REED 1	Piccolo\n\Alto Sax\n\Flute
REED 2	REED 2	Clarinet\n\Tenor Sax
REED 3	REED 3	Bass Clarinet\n\Bari Sax
TRUMPET	Trumpet	(leave blank)
TROMBONE	Trombone	(leave blank)
PIANO	Piano	(leave blank)
BASS	Bass	(leave blank)
DRUMS	Drums	(leave blank)

Input Tempo Text

Every type of text in Sibelius® works in a different way, so it's important to use the right text for each function. We put **Tempo text** in the top left-hand corner of the score to indicate the feel (style) and/or tempo of the piece. Tempo text appears on the score and all the parts. Let's insert this information for *In A Persian Market*:

1. Select the **first bar** of the top instrument in the score (**REED 1** in this case) so that the entire bar is highlighted blue.

2. Type: **Ctrl**+**Alt**+**T** (Mac, type: **T**) to **Create Tempo text**.

3. Type: **Arabic Groove** as the Tempo text. Hit the **space** bar. Type: **Ctrl**+**4** (⌘**4**) on the numpad. Hit the **space** bar and type: **=**, hit the **space** bar and type: **101**.

4. Click outside the text to set it.

   NOTE: For other note values, use the corresponding numpad keys. Example: Type: **5** for a half note.

Tempo text should always go above the time signature in the first bar of the top instrument (*Figure 2.2*). Later in the score, if a new tempo or groove starts on a beat other than the first beat of a bar, select that beat and follow steps 2–4, typing in the appropriate tempo/groove.

Setting up Woodwind Doubles

In Sibelius®, you can view your score in either **Transposed** or **Concert**. For this Lesson, we will use **Transposed**.

Published scores and parts are always transposed. If you want to work in Concert mode, make sure, when you are done with the score, to convert it to Transposed before extracting the Parts. You can toggle between Concert and Transposed by typing: **Ctrl**+**Shift**+**T** (⌘⇧**T**).

NOTE: Woodwind players often double on different reed instruments. This is why, in jazz and commercial music, we use the name **REED 1** instead of a specific instrument. This is similar to a percussion part that includes multiple percussion instruments (Timpani, Triangle, etc.).

When setting up reed books, all the **REED 1** parts go to one player, all the **REED 2** parts to a second player, etc. This eliminates confusion as to who gets which part.

This template uses the most common reed setup in a jazz octet: **REED 1/Alto Sax, REED 2/Tenor Sax, REED 3/Bari Sax**.

NOTE: We use the shorter Sax instead of Saxophone, and Bari instead of Baritone to save space on both the score and parts pages. Let's set these winds up.

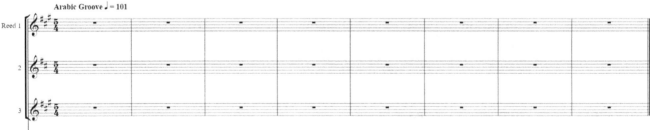

Figure 2.2: Inserting the tempo text.

1. Press **ESC** to make sure nothing is selected. Then type: **Ctrl+Shift+Alt+I** (⌘⇧⌥I) to open the **Instrument Change** menu.

2. Select the box that says **Choose from**: Select **Streamlined Sibelius - Instruments**.

3. Select **Streamlined Sibelius - Instrument family**. Select **Piccolo**.

4. Click anywhere on the first bar of **REED 1** to change it to **Piccolo**.

5. You'll notice that Sibelius® has changed the instrument name on the left. In the left margin, double-click **Piccolo** and rename it **REED 1**.

   Now Sibelius® will recognize that this staff is a **Piccolo** staff, which gives you the correct key signature, octave and MIDI playback—but it says **REED 1**, which is what we prefer to see on the first page of the score and eventually, in the parts.

6. Create the name of the instrument (Piccolo) over **bar 1**. Use **Technique text** by typing: **Ctrl+T** (⌘T). Type: **Piccolo**.

7. If the word **Piccolo** bumps into the Tempo text **Arabic Groove**, select **Arabic Groove** and move it up manually, using the ↑ key.

8. Select the word **Piccolo**. We don't want to see this text on the individual part. To show the instrument in the score, but hide it in the part, use the shortcut **Ctrl+[** (⌘[).

9. Repeat **steps 1–7** for REED 2 and REED 3, using **Clarinet** for REED 2 and **Bass Clarinet** for **REED 3**.

   For Reeds **2** and **3**, we can rename the left margin simply as **2** and **3**. They are already categorized as reed parts.

   Your first bar for the Reeds should look like *Figure 2.3*.

NOTE: Sibelius® normally identifies instruments by their transposition—i.e., **Clarinet in B♭** or **Trumpet in B♭**. In jazz and commercial music, we don't need to say "in B♭" because it is assumed that we are using the most common B♭ clarinet or trumpet.

If a different clarinet is needed, then we have to say which one we mean. For instance, **Bass Clarinet** or in rare cases **E♭ Clarinet** or **E♭ Alto Clarinet**. In our custom instrument menu, **Streamlined Sibelius - Instruments**, we have eliminated these redundancies.

NOTE: To find instruments that are not included in the **Streamlined Sibelius - Instruments** category select the standard Sibelius® instruments menus.

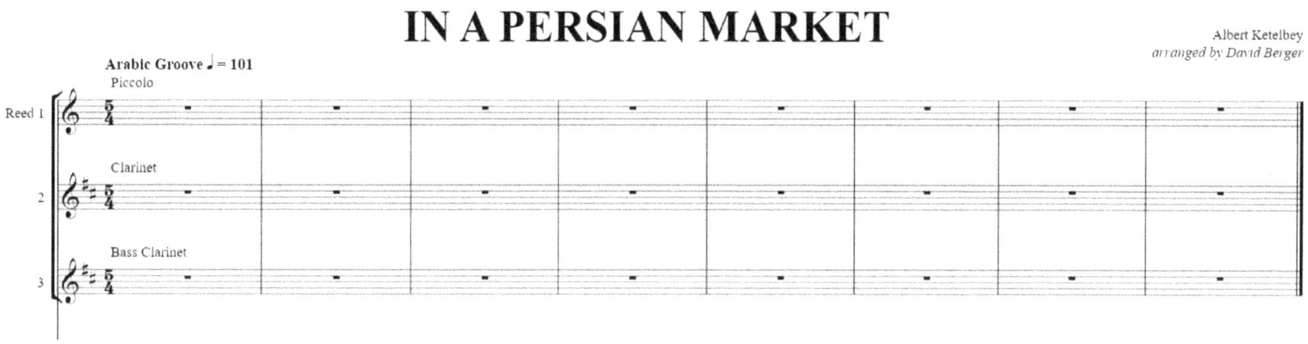

Figure 2.3: First bar for the Reeds.

Setting Up the Page

We have preset Sibelius® to format 8 bars per score page. This works well for most songs, which are constructed in 8-bar phrases. Also, 8 bars provide good spacing, whether the music is busy or sparse.

Since the drum part for this score is quite busy (it uses 16th notes in a 5/4 time signature), we will format the first two pages using 4-bar systems.

1. Select **bars 1–4**.

2. Type **Shift+Alt+M (⌘⌥M)** to **Make Into System**.

NOTE: If you want a different number of bars on a certain page, highlight the top stave for those bars, and select **Make Into System** by typing **Shift+Alt+M (⌘⌥M)**.

This will lock in the selected number of bars *for that page*. Sibelius® will revert to 8 bars per page on the next page. If you want to change the pre-set number of bars per page, go to **Layout > Auto Breaks > System Breaks** and type the desired number of bars in the text box.

Starting phrases on the first bar of each page makes the score look logical to the conductor. It reflects visually what the music sounds like.

Repeat Signs

To create the repeat at the beginning of **bar 1**, press **ESC**, then **right-click (^click)** an empty space on the page. This will open the **Create menu**. Select **Barline > Start Repeat**, and then select **bar 1**.

NOTE: In some older versions of Sibelius®, clicking the bar will place the repeat sign to the *left* of the time signature. If so, click on the time signature and move it a little bit to the left. Then click on the repeat sign and move it to the right of the time signature. Click on a blank space to set.

Inputting the Musical Information

When you are copying a preexisting score, we recommend inputting it one page at a time, from top to bottom—starting with **REED 1** (in this case), and ending with **Drums**. We find this to be the easiest way to keep track of everything we have inputted, and it will likely reduce the number of errors to correct.

Inputting Piano Chords

NOTE: Before you begin, quickly look at the rhythms used in the first four bars of the **Piano** part of *In A Persian Market*. Bars **1**, **2**, and **3** are all rhythmically identical. Only **bar 4** is different.

This is a perfect opportunity to use copy and paste. Input **bar 1**; then copy and paste it into **bars 2** and **3**. Then change the notes as needed. Keep an eye out for opportunities like this. Copy and paste can be a major time saver.

Another option would be to highlight bar one then press shortcut **R** to repeat the selected note, passage or object itself.

1. Input the top voice of the top stave of the **Piano** part for **bar 1**.

2. Copy and paste to **bar 2** and **bar 3**.

3. Go back to **bar 2** and correct all the melody pitches, using the corresponding letter names or the ↑ and ↓ keys on the keyboard. (Don't worry about the cautionary accidentals for now—Sibelius® will fill them in automatically, when we fill in the inner voices.)

   Use the ← and → keys to toggle between each note and/or rest.

4. **Bar 3** is a repeat of **bar 1**; no need to correct any notes.

Inputting Inner Voices by Interval

1. Select the first note in **bar 1** (E).

   We need to create a **C** and a **G** below this. Sibelius® has a great feature that lets you create, *by interval*, a pitch above or below the existing note.

2. Press: **Shift**+**3** (⇧**3**) to create a pitch a diatonic 3rd (in the key) *below* the selected note.

   To create a pitch *above* a given note, you only need to hit the number of the interval above the note (no need to press Shift). So press **2** for an interval a 2nd above, or **5** for a 5th, etc.

   NOTE: For shortcuts, always use *keyboard* numbers, rather than numpad numbers—with the exception of note values in tempo markings.

3. You'll see that a **C** has been created and is now the selected note (highlighted in blue). We now need to create a **G** a 4th below that.

   Press: **Shift**+**4** (⇧**4**).

4. To move to the next chord, press the → arrow key until the **G** on beat **4** is highlighted.

5. This chord has an **E♭** and a **D**. The **E♭** is not a note in the key.

   Press: **Shift**+**3** (⇧**3**) to produce an **E** natural, then press: **9** on the numpad to create the flat.

6. Lastly, we need a **D**. With the **E♭** still selected, press: **Shift**+**2** (⇧**2**) in order to create a note a 2nd below the **E♭** .

7. Continue with this method until the end of Score page 1. (If you look ahead, you'll notice that **bars 1** and **3** are identical—so use copy and paste).

8. For now, wait to input the left hand of the **Piano** until after you input the **Bass**.

Inputting the Bass

Input the **Bass** part as written on the score.

Copy and Paste

We previously left the bass clef of the **Piano** empty. This is a case where looking ahead can save you time. The bottom staff of the **Piano** sounds the same as the **Bass** part but—due to the natural octave transposition of the bass—the **Piano** part must look like it is an octave lower than the **Bass**.

Copy the four bars of the **Bass** part that you just created, and paste them into the bass clef of the **Piano** part. Sibelius® will automatically transpose the notes into the correct octave.

Inputting the Drum Part and Using Two Independent Voices Simultaneously

NOTE: Although drums use the **drum clef**, we treat their notes as if they were in the treble clef. For example, pressing **b** will create a note on the middle line of the staff.

NOTE: We use the following method when writing for drums: Drums and cymbals played with the *hands* are written stems *up*. All drums and cymbals played with the *feet* are written stems *down*. Use the shortcut: **X** to invert stems on selected notes.

Very often in drum parts, two independent lines occur at the same time. We use the **Voices** function to do this. Look at the **Drum** part in **bar 1**.

To recreate this bar:

1. Start with the top part (**Voice 1**) and input the notes as you normally would.

2. Create the cymbal hit on beat **2-*and*** by selecting the note and changing the notehead using **Shift**+**Alt**+**1** (⇧⌥**1**).

   NOTE: Cymbals and rim knocks are both indicated by an **x** notehead. Cymbals are written above the staff. Rim knocks are played on the snare drum and so are notated in the third space of the staff (C).

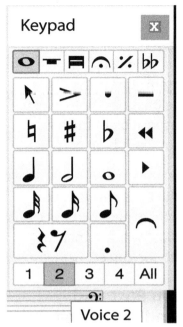

Figure 2.4: Inputting Voice 2 on the Keypad Panel, Step 5.

3. Finish inputting the bar.

4. Press **ESC** to deselect.

5. Now select **Voice 2**, shown in green at the bottom of the **Keypad Panel**. Don't worry about the direction of the stems in **Voice 1**—**Voice 2** will automatically correct that.

   NOTE: Whichever voice is on **top** should be **Voice 1**, and the voice that is on the **bottom** should be **Voice 2**. Otherwise, these two voices will not align correctly.

6. Input the bass drum part as it appears in the score. The first note of **Voice 2** needs to be entered using the cursor.

   Select the **note value** on the numpad. Then click on the appropriate line or space in the staff. After the first note, you can enter other notes by using letter names on the keyboard.

Your **Drum** part should now look like *Figure 2.5*.

7. Using **Technique text** (**Ctrl+T**) (**⌘T**), input the text: Mallets - Snares off. **Deselect (ESC)**.

8. You will need to fix the beaming in **bar 1**, so we can easily see where the beats are. Go to **Keypad Panel 3**.

   With **Keypad Panel 3** open, select the first note (or rest) of each beat and press **7**. Repeat this for each occurrence, then press **ESC**.

   NOTE: For further information on custom beaming, see the ***Sibelius® Reference Guide*** section **Beam Groups**.

9. To create a repeat bar, as in **bar 2**: **Deselect** (**ESC**) and type: **Ctrl+Alt+5** (**⌘⌥5**). Switch back to **Voice 1, and s**elect **bars 2** and **3** to place the repeats.

NOTE: Instead of many slashes in drum parts, we use **repeat bars**. This looks cleaner and makes it easier for drummers to read their parts. The same is true for the guitar, piano and bass, since much of what they play is repetitive. Don't use repeats for other instruments or voice—except for repetitive chord symbols, with slashes, to indicate improvisation.

Creating Rhythmic Slashes

Sibelius® categorizes rhythmic slashes as note-heads. Here's the fastest way to create slashes like we see in bar 4 of the drum part.

1. Input five quarter notes on the middle line (B) of the drum staff.

Figure 2.5: Inputting Voice 2 on the keypad, Step 6.

2. Select the first note and press: **Shift+Alt+4** (⇧⌥**4**). This will change the note to a rhythmic slash with a stem, as seen in the score.

3. Highlight the last four notes of the bar, and press **Shift+Alt+3** (⇧⌥**3**). This will change the remaining notes to stem-less slashes.

   NOTE: Shift+Alt (⇧⌥) plus **a number** is the shortcut we use to modify any notehead. See the *Sibelius® Reference Guide* section **Edit Noteheads** for other available notehead choices.

4. All we have left to enter is the text "Fill" in **bar 4**, which is made up of a combination of **Technique text** and **Lines**. Select the slash on **beat 2**. Press **Ctrl+T** (⌘**T**) and type: **Fill**

5. To create a line, click on beat **3**, and then press **L** to bring up the **Lines Gallery.** Scroll down to the **Brackets** category and select **Bracket above (end)**. This bracket can be adjusted by clicking and dragging its handles manually, or by grabbing the handles and using the ↑, ↓, ←, or → arrows.

NOTE: Most objects in Sibelius® have handles you can "grab," represented by blue or purple squares. Handles are hidden until selected. Clicking and dragging them lets you modify and manipulate objects. To see all the handles available in your score, in the Ribbon, select **View > Invisibles > Handles**. Now uncheck **Handles** to hide them (they still remain usable). Keeping them visible can crowd the workspace.

6. Click in the center of the bracket and drag it upward, till it lines up with the tops of the letters in the word **Fill**. (Be sure not to engage the handles.)

Now click the handle on the right side of the bracket, and drag it to the right until it lines up with the barline.

Inputting Dynamics

The final piece of information to enter on page 1 is the dynamic *mf* in each of the rhythm section parts.

1. In a two-handed **Piano** part, if the dynamics are the same for both hands, we place the dynamic between the staves by attaching it to the correct beat in the treble clef.

   Select the eighth rest on beat **1** of the treble clef of the **Piano**, as well as the **Bass** and **Drums**, by pressing and holding **Control** (⌘) while selecting all three.

2. Use **Ctrl+E** (⌘**E**) to create **Expression text**.

3. Hold down **Ctrl** (⌘) and type: **mf**. Sibelius® will automatically choose the proper font and size.

4. You can apply the same dynamic to other instruments by using the cut and paste method.

   NOTE: To apply similar dynamic text to a group of instruments, hold down **Shift**, and select the bar or note to apply the dynamic to for each instrument. Then follow **Step 2** above. The dynamic will be applied to all the instruments at once. This is very helpful for *tutti* sections for large ensemble and many other purposes.

   NOTE: After pressing **Ctrl+E** (⌘**E**) to create **Expression text**, right-click (^**click**) to see an exhaustive list of expression options. This is a great menu to familiarize yourself with.

Figure 2.6: Inputting technique text, rhythmic slashes, brackets, and dynamics.

IN A PERSIAN MARKET

Albert Ketelbey
arranged by David Berger

6/1/2021

Figure 2.7: Page 1 of the octet score, completed.

5. You should now have all the information you need to complete inputting page 1. The completed page should look like Figure 2.7.

Score Page 2

1. Click on an empty space on page 1 and scroll to the right until page 2 appears. Sibelius® will automatically have put the extra 4 bars that you didn't use on page 1, onto this page. Again, for the sake of the drum part for this score, we will limit page 2 to a 4-bar system.

2. Since we have preset 8 bars per page, select the first 4 bars on this page and type: **Shift+Alt+M (⇧⌥M)** to **Make Into System**.

Inputting Winds and Brass

The winds and brass only play one note on this page—an eighth note on the *and* of beat **5** in **bar 8**. If we were to input each horn part that way, entering all the rests, we would waste a lot of time. So we input one instrument, and copy and paste that part into all the instruments with a similar rhythm. After that, we can make changes as needed. Let's input the brass and winds.

1. Input the rests and the note **E** in the **REED 1** part.

2. Input the *mf* dynamic.

3. Input: *Tacet 1st x* over the 8th rest at the beginning of the bar by clicking on the dotted half rest and using **Technique text Ctrl+T (⌘T)**.

NOTE: The preferred method is over the first note of the tacet section, but the beginning of the measure may be preferable to avoid clutter.

NOTE: In music we use Italian terms, hence *tacet* instead of the Latin/English tacit.

NOTE: We generally give directions for what happens the first time, rather than something like "Play 2nd x only." Seeing "play" as the first word can be confusing when sight-reading.

4. Now, instead of inputting rests, dynamics and Tacet information all over again, just copy and paste the *REED 1* part into the other horns.

Since the horns are in harmony, the pitches will be incorrect. Change the pitch using the method discussed on p. 28.

NOTE: When pasting similar information into multiple parts, select all the bars you want to copy. Select the **first bar** you want to paste to, and press **Ctrl+V (⌘V)**.

You only need to click the first bar or—if you are replacing other notes—the first note, not the whole section.

For instance, after copying **bar 8** in **REED 1**, click **bar 8** in the **REED 2** part. Hold down **Shift**, click in **bar 8** of the **Trombone** part, and press **Ctrl+V (⌘V)**.

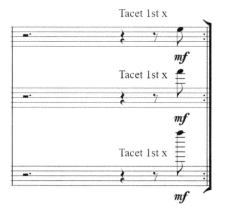
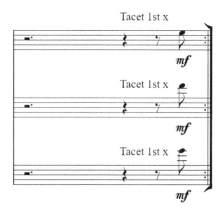

Figure 2.8: Copy and paste Reed Part 1 into Reed Parts 2 and 3. Then adjust the pitches.

5. Note that the **Trumpet** and **Trombone** are using cup mutes. Click the *Tacet 1st x* text in the **Trumpet** part to edit it. Press **Enter** (**Return**) and type: **Cup Mute**. This shortcut allows you to edit any previously entered text type. If the *Cup Mute* text bumps into the staff, select and move it, using the ↑ key.

6. Repeat **step 5** for the **Trombone**.

   NOTE: When you add *Tacet* to an instrument, Sibelius® will mute that instrument *during that section* in the playback. A Tacet ends when the next change of dynamic takes place. Here, we only want the Tacet to apply to the first time through this section. So:

   Select the text: *Tacet 1st x*, then type **Ctrl+Shift+I** (⌘⇧I) to open the **Inspector** menu. Once the Inspector is open, at the bottom under **Playback**, you'll see options for **Play on Pass**. Keep **1** checked, but *uncheck* **2** by clicking on it. That way, the Tacet will only happen on the first pass through, not the second.

Changing Clef in the Piano Part

1. In **bar 5**, you'll find that the right hand of the **Piano** shifts to the bass clef. In order to change the clef, first press **ESC** to deselect.

2. Highlight the Barline at the end of measure 4 (where the bass clef begins), and type shortcut **Q** to access the **Clef menu**.

3. Select **Bass clef** from the menu.

4. In **bar 7**, repeat the same process, changing back to **Treble clef**.

Finish Inputting Page 2

You should now have all the information you need to finish inputting the rest of page 2. Do that now, before moving on to page 3. The completed page 2 should look like *Figure 2.9*.

Score Page 3

You now know how to do about 90 percent of the inputting required in this score: notes, text, rhythmic slashes, chord symbols, drum notation and more. Next, we'll discuss a few new things you will need to input page 3.

1. To create the new page, highlight the last bar of any instrument on page 2. Type shortcut **Alt+B** (⌥B) to **Add New Bars**. Type in **5** (the number of bars you want to add) and select **OK** or press **Enter** (**Return**).

2. Again, we have preset 8 bars per page. To create page 3 with a 5-bar system, highlight these 5 bars and type: **Shift+Alt+M** (⇧⌥M).

Change Time Signature (Meter Signature)

1. Press **ESC** to deselect.

2. Press **T** to open the **Time Signature** menu.

3. Select **4/4**.

4. Place this time signature over **bar 1** (the first bar of this page).

Rehearsal Letters

To create a rehearsal letter A : Click **bar 1** (or the bar you would like to place it over) and press **Ctrl+R** (⌘R). Sibelius® will create a new rehearsal letter, in alphabetical order, each time you do this.

NOTE: In our template, we have disabled bar numbering. In our experience, it is unnecessary, clutters the page, and distracts both conductors and performers. A rehearsal letter (or number) every 8 bars or so is sufficient to mark the form.

Letters (or numbers) should occur at the beginnings of **sections**, along with double bars. This matches the score visually to what is heard.

We refer to **bars** by their rehearsal letter and bar number. For example, **A1** is the first bar of letter **A**, and **G5** is the fifth bar of letter **G**.

Figure 2.9: Page 2 of the octet score, completed.

NOTE: We prefer rehearsal letters to numbers; they are easier to communicate than 2- or 3-digit numbers. For long pieces, after letter **Z**, Sibelius® will automatically continue with double letters (**AA**, **BB**, **CC**). Triple letters can be unwieldy, so, for very long pieces, numbers may be preferable.

To make the form clear, we usually put letter **A** after the Introduction. When referring to bars in the **Intro**, we just give the bar number, or we can say, "Intro bar 5." (For Intros longer than 15 bars, we use **A** at the first bar of the Intro).

To use rehearsal numbers instead of letters: In the **Ribbon**, select **Appearance > Engraving Rules > Rehearsal Marks**. In the next menu, you will find several options for Rehearsal Marks.

Position Rehearsal Marks

Plug-in Download: Before starting **Lesson 1**, you should have downloaded the Plug-in, but if you didn't, do it now:

1. With any Sibelius® file open, click on **File** and, under the drop-down menu, select **Plug-ins > Install Plug-ins**.

2. A new window will open. Select **Show > All Plug-ins**.

3. Scroll down and then select: **Text**.

4. A third window, with a drop-down menu, will open. With this menu open, select: **Position Rehearsal Marks**, then click on **Install** at the bottom right, directly above **Close**.

5. Click **Close** to close the windows. The plug-in will be installed and you can use it on any Sibelius® file. (Our thanks to **Bob Zawalich** for this, and many other wonderful plug-ins that maximize Sibelius's capabilities!)

6. Open the plug-in it by typing: **Ctrl+Alt+P** (⌘⌥P). Input these settings:

   • For each file processed, change: **Full Score and Dynamic Parts**.

   • Extra spaces to shift left (**–**) or right (**+**): **1 character = –1**

Select **Current Score** to apply the plug-in to both score and parts in the current file.

NOTE: Sibelius® does not let you move more than one rehearsal mark at a time. This plug-in allows you to move all the rehearsal marks in a piece at once. Whether you're writing for small ensembles or symphony orchestras, this helpful plug-in can save you a lot of time!

Inserting the Segno (𝄋)

1. Highlight bar **A1**.

2. Right click on a a blank space outside of the staff to open the **Create menu.**

3. Click on **Text > Other System Text > Repeat (D.C./D.S./To Coda) Signs**. (This should be at the bottom of the menu under **User Defined**). Do not select **Repeat (D.C./D.S./To Coda)**—that is used only for repeat text, and the Signs option can be used for all symbols.

4. **Right-click** (**^click**) on a blank space.

5. Select the desired **Segno** from the menu.

6. Click on a blank space or deselect (**ESC**) to set it.

7. Click and drag the **Segno** into the desired position.

Inserting the Coda Sign (⊕)

The coda sign is located in the same menu as the Segno, so follow the same steps as above. Here, you must highlight the barline, rather than the full bar. Choose the appropriate coda symbol and move it into place manually.

Grace Notes

In bar **A1**, there are a few grace notes in the **Piccolo** part. To create grace notes:

1. Create an 8th note **G#** on beat **1**.

2. Click on the note and type a semicolon (**;**) to turn it into a grace note.

3. With the grace note still selected, press shortcut **/** to turn it into a slashed grace note (acciaccatura).

4. Create quarter note **A**.

5. Copy and paste beat **1** onto beats **2** and **3**.

6. Input the rest of the **Piccolo** part for this page. Notice that the **Piano** part is in a 2-octave unison with the **Piccolo**. (The **Piccolo** sounds an octave above where written.) Copy and paste the **Piccolo** part onto the **Piano's** top stave. With the pasted notes still highlighted, type **Ctrl+↓↓** (**⌘↓↓**) to transpose them down two octaves.

Inputting Notes—Copy and Paste

Since most objects attach to notes, input the notes for the entire page before you add text, phrase marks, and articulations. These add-ons can take time and interrupt your workflow.

That said, if there are objects that appear on multiple parts, it is usually best to input the notes for the top part and add the objects before copying and pasting to other parts.

Just as the **Piccolo** and right hand of the **Piano** are in unison, the **Bass Clarinet**, left hand of the **Piano** and **String Bass** are also in unison. Sibelius® will make the octave transposition for you, so you can just copy and paste (see *Figure 2.10*). There is one extra note in the **Bass Clarinet** on the *and* of beat **4** in bar **A4**—be sure to add it.

Similarly, the **Trombone** part has the same rhythms (though not pitches) as the **Trumpet**. Input the **Trumpet** part, copy and paste it to the **Trombone** stave, and adjust the pitches for the **Trombone**. This leaves just the **Clarinet** and **Drums** to be input separately.

Articulations

Add articulations the same way as you would a flat or sharp. Select the articulation on the **Keypad Panel** before you place the note. Or click on the note after placing it, and then select the articulation. The most common articulations are on the **Keypad Panel 1**; less common ones are on **Keypad Panels 2–6**. It is helpful to get familiar with each menu and its contents.

Slurs and Phrase Markings

To create a **slur** as in the REED 2 (**Clarinet**) part:

1. Highlight the notes under the slur.

2. Press shortcut **S**.

3. Another way to add slurs: Input the first note, then hit **S**, and type all the pitches in the slurred phrase, followed by **ESC**. Press the → arrow key to move to the next note before inputting new notes not under that slur.

NOTE: Slurs can be adjusted by clicking and dragging one of their handles. Occasionally, slurs don't behave as expected because of the program's magnetic layout, which automatically determines the spacing between staves. It may help to **right-click (^click)** the slur and select **Magnetic Layout > Off**.

You should now have all the information you need to input the rest of page 3. Do it now before moving on to page 4. The completed page 3 should look like *Figure 2.11*.

Figure 2.10: The Bass Clarinet part is copied and pasted into the left hand of the Piano, and the Bass.

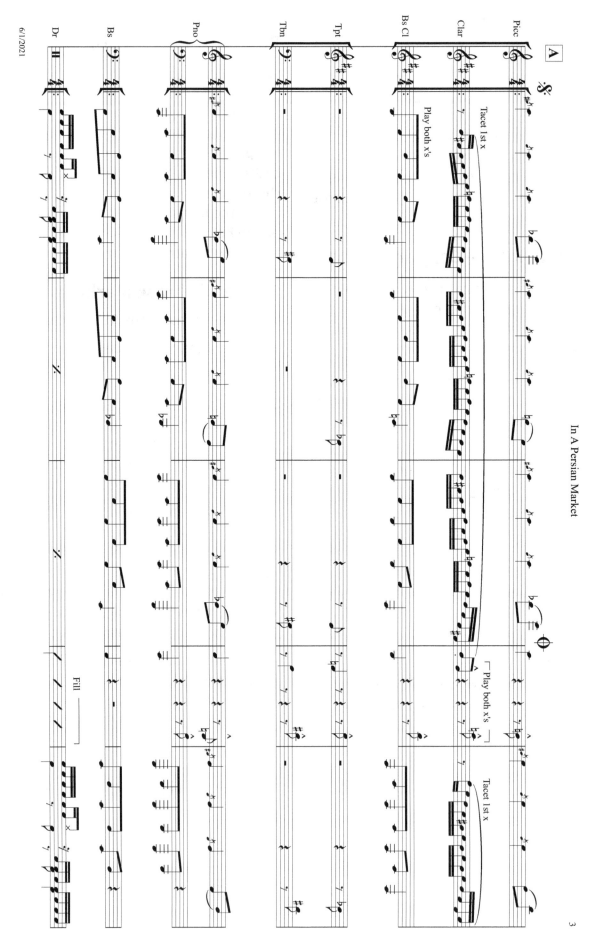

Figure 2.11: Page 3 of the octet score, completed.

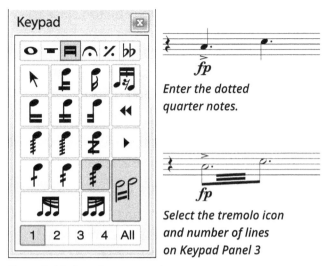

Enter the dotted quarter notes.

Select the tremolo icon and number of lines on Keypad Panel 3

Figure 2.12: Creating a tremolo.

Score Page 4

1st and 2nd Endings

1. To indicate a first ending: In the top staff of the page, select bar **A8**, which becomes the **1st ending**.

2. Use shortcut **L** to open the **Lines Gallery.**

3. Select **Repeat Endings > 1st Ending**.

4. The **1st Ending** text (**1.**) and the horizontal bracket will appear over the 1st ending, above the top staff.

5. Highlight both bars of the **2nd ending** in the top staff. From the **Lines Gallery**, select **Repeat Endings > 2nd Ending**.

6. If necessary, adjust the length and height of the brackets by clicking and dragging them or their handles.

   NOTE: You only need to indicate 1st and 2nd endings once, in the top staff of the score. They will automatically appear on all the parts.

Tremolo

In bar **A8**, the **Clarinet** plays a tremolo:

1. Input the notes as dotted quarter notes (see *Figure 2.12*).

2. Highlight both notes.

3. In **Keypad Panel 3**, press **Enter** to select the icon for **Tremolo with next note**. In the same menu, to the left of the tremolo icon, select how many lines you want between the two notes (in this case, 3) by pressing **3** on the numpad.

Fixing the Clarinet Slur

The **Clarinet** slur that starts on page 3, bar **A5** and ends in the first bar of the **2nd ending** (page 4, bar **A9**) should be created after all the notes are put in.

1. Sibelius® cannot continue a slur through a **1st ending**. So, end the slur on the final note before the **1st ending**.

   Using the right-most handle of the slur, raise the slur slightly, to show that it will continue through to the **2nd ending**.

2. The next step can be done in one of two ways, depending on which version of Sibelius® you have.

   Sibelius® 2020.1 or newer:

   • Select the first note in the **2nd ending**.

   • Using **Keypad Panel 4**, hit **Enter** on the numpad to tie the end of the slur to this note.

   Versions before 2020.1:

   • Deselect (**ESC**).

   • Press **S** to load your cursor with a slur.

   • Click near (but not on) the spot where you want to place the slur. This will create a slur that does not attach to a specific note (it appears red when selected).

   • Click and drag the slur handles until it is shaped and placed properly (use the score as a guide).

Instrument Change

1. **Reeds 1, 2** and **3** have an **Instrument Change** in bar **A10**. To put in the **REED 1** change, deselect (**ESC**).

2. Type **Ctrl+Shift+Alt+I** (⌘⇧⌥I) to open the **Instrument Change** menu.

3. From the **Streamlined Sibelius - Instrument Family** category, select **Alto Sax**. *Uncheck* **Announce at last note of previous instrument** (at the bottom of the window)—the extra warning is not needed here.

Click on bar **A10** in the top staff. The new key signature will appear at the beginning of this bar, and the new instrument name will appear over the first note played.

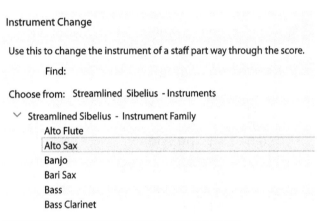

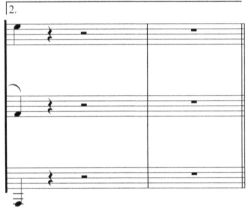

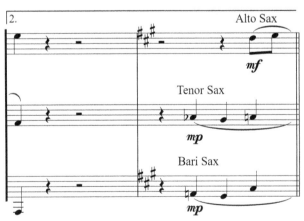

Figure 2.13: Inputting instrument changes.

4. The new key signature may be too close to the left barline. (This spacing issue has been corrected in Sibelius® 8.7.2 and later versions.) For previous versions, highlight bar **A10** and press **Ctrl+Shift+N** (⌘⇧N) to fix it.

5. Repeat **steps 1–4** for **Reeds 2** and **3**, using **Tenor Sax** and **Bari Sax** from the **Instrument Change** menu. (See *Figure 2.13*.)

You should now have all the information needed to input the rest of page 4. Do it now before moving on to page 5. The completed page 4 should look like *Figure 2.14*.

Score Page 5

Creating a Scoop (⌒)

Create the new page with an 11-bar system.

In bar **B6** of the **REED 1** part, the F# has a scoop approaching it. Open **Keypad Panel 5** and press **7** on the numpad. That attaches the scoop to the F#.

Entering Chord Symbols with Slashes

1. In **B1**, the **Piano** has chord symbols over slashes. To make the slashes, enter middle line quarter note **D's** in the bass clef.

2. Highlight the notes and type **Shift+Alt+3** (⇧⌥3) to change the noteheads to slashes.

3. With the first slash in **B1** highlighted, press **Ctrl+K** (⌘K).

4. Type in the chord names, using the space bar or tab key to move the cursor to the proper spot for the next chord symbol.

5. To make slashes for transposing instruments: Input pitches that, when transposed, would sound like the middle line **B** for the treble clef, or the middle line **D** for the bass clef. Thus for **Alto Sax** you would use **G's** on top of the staff (a 6th above middle line **B**), and for **Baritone Sax**, you'd use **G's** an octave above that.

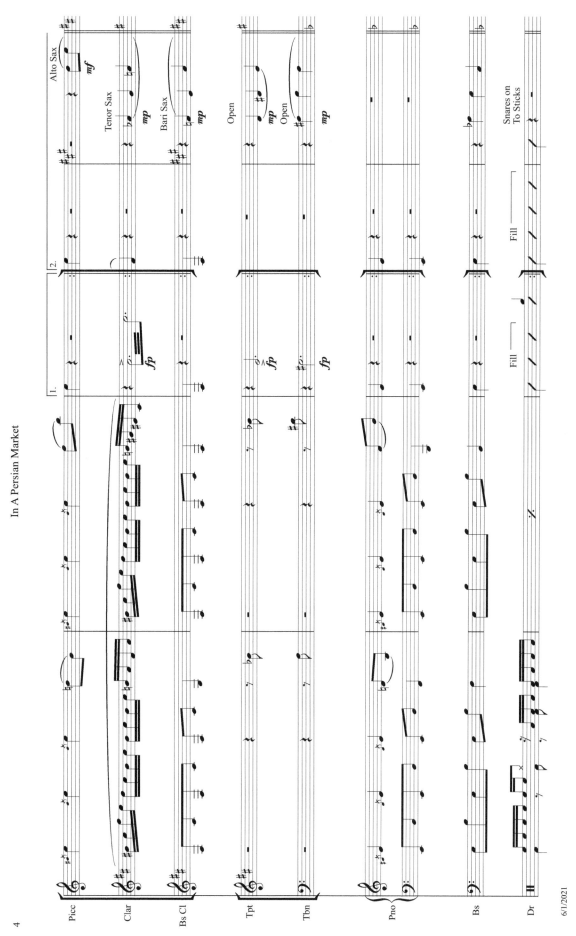

Figure 2.14: Page 4 of the octet score, completed.

In **B10** and **B11** the **Trumpet** has 6 beats of **D7–9**. Since the **Piano** chord begins a beat earlier, it cannot be copied onto the **Trumpet** part. So you must create the **Trumpet** part separately for these two bars:

1. Create a **half rest**, followed by 6 third-space **C** quarter notes. Since the **Trumpet** transposes up a step, we need to accommodate that step.

2. Select the first **C** quarter note and type: **Ctrl+K** (⌘**K**).

3. Type **C,7,–,9**. Sibelius® will transpose up a step to the proper **Trumpet** key.

4. Highlight these 2 bars and type: **Shift+Alt+3** (⇧⌥**3**) to create slashes.

   NOTE: We prefer to delete the rests in the treble clef when the pianist is soloing or comping, to allow space for the pianist to write in any desired information.

   NOTE: When you enter the text: **Harmon mute - Solo**, Sibelius® wants to place the text below the chord symbol. Click and drag this text so that it appears *above* the chord symbol. Chord symbols should always be the closest text to the staff.

   NOTE: On **versions 2019.4** and later, when you cut and paste chord symbols and slashes from one instrument to another, they will automatically transpose into the correct position.

Creating a Decrescendo/Crescendo

To create the **decrescendo** (**diminuendo**) in the **Rhythm** section parts in bar **B11**:

1. Highlight the bar.

2. Hold **Shift** and type **H** (for "Hairpin").

   (To create a **crescendo**, highlight a bar and type **H**.)

At this point, you should know almost all you need to copy pages 6–10. The last few things to cover can be found below.

Score Pages 6–10

Double Dotted Notes

In bar **C1** we use double dotted half notes. To create a double dotted half note, select the beat you want to apply the note to. Type **5** on **Keypad Panel 1** (half note), then press the **+** sign on the numpad, which will take you to **Keypad Panel 2**. Once here, type **2** on the numpad. Then enter the desired pitch. Deselect (**ESC**).

Custom Repeat Ending

In bar **D8** we need an ending that reads: **1, 2, etc.** and in bar **D9**, an ending that reads: **Last x**. We have already created these custom lines for you. You'll find them in the **Lines Gallery**. Highlight the bars in the ending, type **L**, scroll down to the ending that reads **1, 2, etc.** and click on it.

8va (Octave Higher)

To input an **8va** symbol, as in bar **F7** in the **Piano** and **Bass** parts: Select all the notes involved and press **L**. Scroll down to where it says **Octave Lines** and select **Octave up (8va)**. If necessary, use the handles to adjust the length and/or height of the line.

D.S. al Coda

At **F10** there is a **D.S. al Coda**. To create and insert it:

1. **Right-click** (**^click**) on a blank space outside the staff.

2. In the **Create menu**, click on **Text > Other System Text > Repeat (D.C./D.S./To Coda)** (at the top of the menu under **Common**).

   NOTE: Don't click on **Repeat (D.C./D.S./To Coda) Signs**—that is used only for symbols, while the above selection is used only for text.

3. Click on the right barline of **F10**. **Right-click** (**^click**) on a blank space.

4. Select the **D.S. al Coda** from the menu.

5. Click on a blank space, or deselect (**ESC**) to set it.

Shortening the Staves for Short (Final) Score Pages

On page 10, you will want to lessen the width of the staves, since there are only three bars on this page.

1. Select bar **F10**, the last barline on page 9.

2. Create a Special Page Break: Type **Ctrl**+**Shift**+**Enter** (⌘⇧**Return**).

3. In the **Special Page Break** menu, *uncheck* the box marked **Blank Pages**.

4. Select **New Margins** and click on **Margins**.

5. In the **Margins** menu, select **Page Margins > Left Pages.** In the center-right field, enter **160** as the **Value**.

   NOTE: This controls the right margin. Increasing the number widens the margin. (You may need to change the number depending on the size of a score and the number of bars on a page).

Figure 2.15: Shortening the staves for the short final page, Special Page Break menu and Margins menu. See results, next page.

NOTE: NEVER DRAG MARGIN HANDLES! Always use the above process when changing page margins. Dragging the margins in the score can cause unintended, catastrophic results in the parts.

Pulling In the Repeat Bar

One point worth mentioning is the look of the 5/4 time signature and the repeat section at the end of the piece. Call us picky, but we like score pages to look clean and uncluttered. Pulling the starting repeat to the left, so it overlaps with the barline, brings it even with the 5/4 time signature and gives the page a nice clean look (see *Figure 2.17*).

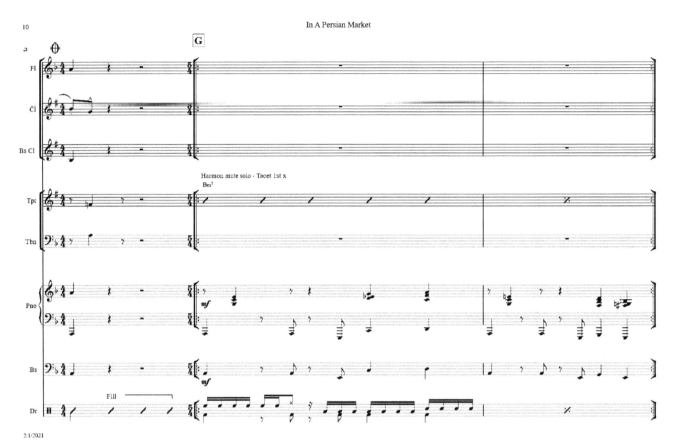

Figure 2.16a: Page 10 before shortening the staves.

Figure 2.16b: Page 10 after shortening the staves.

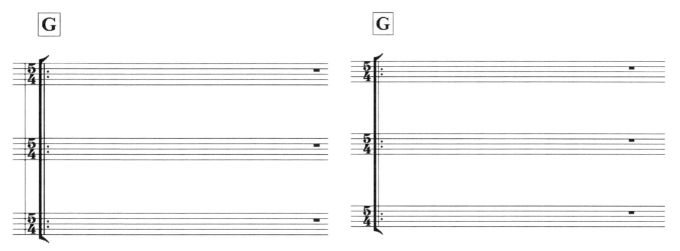

Figure 2.17: Pulling in the repeat bar.

To do this, select the repeat. Then press the ← arrow until the repeat overlaps the barline. You may need to zoom in close to make sure you get the best alignment possible.

Formatting

Formatting begins after you input all the notes, lyrics, chord symbols, and any other markings needed in the score. It takes your score from merely legible to publisher-ready.

This is a step that many Sibelius® users overlook. Sibelius® does an extremely good job of formatting much of your work, but it's up to you to do the last bit. Here's our step-by-step process.

We'll assume that you have used all of our templates and House Style. (We've worked for years to develop them in order to reduce the number of steps required during setup and formatting.)

Sibelius® Auto-formatting

You've already learned about using **Reset Note Spacing** and **Optimize Staff Spacing** in **Lesson 1** (p. 18).

NOTE: Reset Note Spacing will undo **pulling in the repeat bar** as described above, so:
Either wait until the end to pull in the repeat

bar, or don't select bar **G1** when you reset the note spacing.

After you use **Optimize Staff Spacing**, if any staves are not spaced vertically as you would like, click and drag them manually to the desired position. Click on a blank space in the staff to select the entire stave, and then drag it up or down.

NOTE: If you've taken all of these steps, and staves still look too close to each other, try reducing the staff size: In the **Ribbon**, select **Layout > Staff Size**.

Use this function only as a last resort, though. It will make your staves smaller, along with the notes and some of the text elements. Conversely, if the staves and notes are too small and there is too much white space on a page, you can make the staves larger.

Proofing

Always proof your work! Repeat: *PROOF YOUR WORK.* We cannot stress this enough. Our main goal in engraving music is to reduce the number of questions that musicians have to ask at rehearsal. Questions eat up time, and time is money. Proofing your work is well worth the extra time and energy.

Proof with Your Eyes

This goes without saying. Spend time reading every note and symbol of the score to make sure there are no mistakes.

Here is our **Checklist**, which will keep you focused on one thing at a time. As much as we all think that we can multitask, no one can give 100 percent attention to more than one thing at a time—and less than 100 percent invites errors. You may want to keep this list handy on your desk while you proof.

PROOFING CHECKLIST

▸ **Double Bars at every Rehearsal Mark.** Helps both conductor and players organize the form and keep their place in the music.

▸ **Piano Part:** No rests in the treble clef when chord symbols are accompanied by slashes in the bass clef. Lets the player pencil in information.

▸ **Enharmonic:**

1. Sharps when ascending, flats when descending. This goes for chord symbols as well.

2. In chromatic music, make the passage look like it is in a key (as much as possible).

3. Opt for fewer accidentals.

4. Avoid awkward-looking intervals and more than one chromatic use of the same pitch (where possible).

5. Avoid double sharps and flats. Be on the lookout for them when transposing.

▸ **Hide player-specific information from the score**—conductors don't need to know instrument changes until the first note. Ditto word cues and numbers over repeated bars.

▸ **Rehearsal Marks over Clefs** Use the Rehearsal Mark Plug-in. Letters directly over clefs and barlines leave more space for notes and text.

▸ Make sure that your **headers** appear where they should.

▸ Reposition the **copyright notice** if it is too close or too far from the bottom stave on page 1. Also, it shouldn't be too close to the bottom of the page, or it may be cut off when the page is printed.

Proof with Your Ears (Playback)

At the end of a project, always do a playback of the score. To start a playback, type **Ctrl+Alt+Y** (⌘⌥Y) to open the **Transport** panel. The **Transport** lets you scroll to wherever you want in the score, and starts the playback from there, when you press the **Play** button.

Use the slider next to the metronome icon in the **Transport** Panel to change the playback speed. Reduce the tempo to give the playback your full attention. Listening to your score will reveal mistakes that your eyes may have overlooked.

It is easy to overlook wrong pitches, accidentals, and rhythms—for example, a **C#** in a **C major** chord. That kind of dissonance might be overlooked by your eyes, but your ears can't miss it. Another frequent mistake that will be obvious on the playback is if a figure appears in the wrong bar, or is missing.

Your Score Is Finished—

Time to move on to formatting the individual instrumental parts.

Lesson 2 Shortcuts Quick Reference

Ctrl+Shift+T (⌘⇧T)	Toggle between **Concert and Transposed Score**		**Shift+Alt+1** (⇧⌥1)	Create an **x notehead** (useful for cymbals).
S	**Slur** to next note, or slur a group of notes.		**Shift+Alt+4** (⇧⌥4)	Change note to a **specific rhythmic slash**.
Ctrl+Shift+Alt+I (⌘⇧⌥I)	Open **Instrument Change** menu		**Shift+Alt+3** (⇧⌥3)	Change note to a non-specific **stem-less slash**.
Ctrl+Alt+T (⌘⌥T)	Create **Tempo text**.		**Shift+Alt** (⇧⌥) **plus a number**	Change a note to one of many types of **noteheads.**
Ctrl+3 (⌘3) on numpad	Create an **eighth note** in Tempo text.		**;**	Turn a note into a **grace note.***
Ctrl+4 (⌘4) on numpad	Create a **quarter note** in Tempo text.		**/**	Turn a grace note into a **slashed grace note.***
Ctrl+5 (⌘5) on numpad	Create a **half note** in Tempo text.		**L**	Open **Lines Gallery**.
T	Open **Time Signature** menu.		**Ctrl+Shift+I** (⌘⇧I)	Open **Inspector menu**.
Ctrl+T (⌘T)	Create **Technique text**.		**Ctrl+E** (⌘E)	Create **Expression text**.
Shift+Alt+M (⇧⌥M)	Make selected bars into a **system** (how many in a staff)		**Q**	Create a **new Clef**.
Ctrl+[(⌘[)	Show information in **score**, but not in parts.*		**Ctrl+R** (⌘R)	Create a **Rehearsal Mark**.
Ctrl+] (⌘])	Show information in **parts**, but not in score.*		**H**	Create a **crescendo** hairpin sign.
Ctrl+Alt+5 (⌘⌥5)	Create a **Repeat Bar.***		**Shift+H** (⇧H)	Create a **diminuendo** (decrescendo) hairpin sign.
X	**Invert stems** of selected notes.		**Ctrl+Shift+Enter** (⌘⇧Return)	Create a **Special Page Break** at selected barline.
Create a simultaneous vertical pitch **above** a note in the same staff: Select note, then type the number of the **interval** (2,3,4, etc.).			**Ctrl+Shift+N** (⌘⇧N)	**Reset Note Spacing**.
Create a simultaneous vertical pitch **below** a note in same staff: Select note, then hold down **Shift** and type the number of the **interval** (2,3,4, etc.).			**Ctrl+Alt+S** (⌘⌥S)	**Optimize Staff Spacing.***
Ctrl+Alt+Y (⌘⌥Y)	Open **Transport** panel.			

* Not standard with Sibelius®. To install, see pp. 6–9.
** See *Sibelius® Reference Guide* for additional information.

Lesson 3. Creating Parts

Formatting parts is one of the best reasons to use Sibelius®. This chapter will take you through the various steps and techniques for extracting and formatting parts. Your goal is to make the cleanest and most logical-looking parts for musicians—since poor engraving and/or formatting will cause problems that waste valuable rehearsal time.

What Not to Do

Some Sibelius® users create separate files for scores and parts. This subverts one of the greatest advantages of the program: We *want* the score and parts to be linked! It saves time in creating and editing parts, and it produces a more organized library of Sibelius® scores.

Sibelius® doesn't just speed up notating music; it speeds up the whole engraving process. Most of the copying rules and decisions that copyists make are done by the program.

But that doesn't mean all of the details will be correct and optimal for every situation—and you still have to know the standard rules of notation. A composer will spend hours, days or even weeks writing, arranging and orchestrating a score, making sure the notation is clear and concise.

With the score of *In A Persian Market* finished, formatted and ready to go, let's look at a sample

REED 1 part automatically generated *without* using our House Style. Picture yourself as a musician reading this part at a rehearsal. (See *Figure 3.1* on the next page).

This is *not* music that a musician would enjoy playing. Without proper engraving conventions, it is difficult to understand and keep your place in the music. With poorly formatted parts, the composer/arranger is unlikely to get a good reading of the piece. The whole ensemble will be frustrated because, instead of focusing on musical issues, they will be trying to piece together the road map.

Our House Style

Using our House Style solves about 90 percent of the issues (see *Figure 3.2*). This is much better, but still needs a little work. The next version (see *Figure 3.3*) is our finished part.

To complete this part, you need to know a few basic engraving concepts. In this lesson, you will create a set of parts for *In A Persian Market* and cover all the situations that arise in this chart.

To view the complete finished parts, open the Resources folder and open **Streamlined-Sibelius_Charts.zip**. The parts are on pages 12–28 of the pdf.

(continued p. 52)

IN A PERSIAN MARKET

Figure 3.1: REED 1 part without House Style or corrections.

REED 1
Piccolo
Alto Sax
Flute

IN A PERSIAN MARKET

Albert Ketelby
arranged by David Berger

Figure 3.2: REED 1 part with House Style, some correction needed.

REED 1
Piccolo
Alto Sax
Flute

IN A PERSIAN MARKET

Albert Ketelbey
arranged by David Berger

Figure 3.3: REED 1 part with House Style and corrections.

How Sibelius® Makes Extracting Parts Easy

One of Sibelius's greatest assets is how easy it makes extracting parts from scores. In early versions, the user had to extract each part to its own file. Any changes to the score or parts had to be made both in the score and in each individual part.

Recent versions have the score and parts linked, and all contained in one .sib file. The software transfers almost all of the changes from the score to the parts, and vice versa. Most of the time, Sibelius® coordinates the score and parts so as not to disturb any previous formatting. But, since this doesn't work perfectly every time, it's important to understand how the program thinks, so you can spot and correct any problems that arise.

Preparation

Although there are many ways to extract parts, we will show you our process, which, if done in this precise order, will save time, energy and stress down the road.

Parts Drop-Down Menu

The **Parts Drop-Down Menu** is located at the top right of your workstation (the + sign, *Figure 3.4*). When you click it, you'll find that Sibelius® has created an individual part for each instrument in your score.

NOTE: If you haven't yet input the **Instrument Changes** described on pp. 39–40, do it now.

NOTE: There is a plug-in called **Open Selected Parts** that lets you open all the parts at once. You should have installed it before working through **Lesson 1**. If you haven't, open to p. 6 and go through the steps to install it.

Type **Ctrl+Alt+Shift+O** (⌘⌥⇧**O**) to open this plug-in. Once opened, press **Ctrl+A** (⌘**A**) to select all parts, then press **OK** or **Enter** (**Return**). With the plug-in open, when you are in the **parts view** you can quickly switch from part to part by pressing **Ctrl+Tab** (⌘**Tab**).

Open Selected Parts   Version 01.22.00

Click or ctrl/cmnd-click on a part name to select or unselect it. Selected parts will be opened (or will remain open) in a tab; unselected parts will be closed.

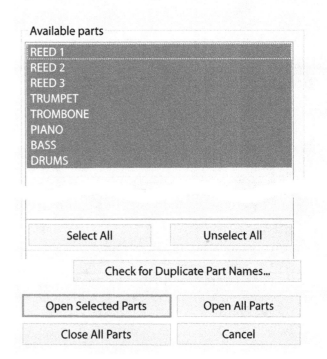

Figure 3.4: Two ways to open parts: the Parts drop-down menu and the Open Selected Parts plug-in.

Formatting the Parts

Our **Manuscript Paper** is preset for 4 bars to a line (system). This spacing shows visually what is happening audibly in music that is mostly written in 4-bar phrases. Most of the time, 4-bar systems look good on a printed page. The exceptions are when you have 8 bars of whole notes, multi-bar rests, a lot of 16th notes, or wordy lyrics that require fewer than 4 bars per line.

Let's go through and set up some system breaks for *In A Persian Market.* This is where you need to use your own judgment as to what looks most legible and what follows the phrases in the music. In places, you'll have to compromise.

Page Layout Guidelines– Where to Put the Breaks

- Whenever possible, keep **Rehearsal Marks in the left margin**.

- **Page Turns:** If a part includes more than 3 pages, plan for page turns by leaving enough rest/s at the bottom of the previous page or at the top of the next page.

  This may be impossible for the rhythm section, since they often play in every bar. If possible, squeeze the **Guitar**, **Bass**, and **Drum** parts so they fit onto 3 or fewer pages.

  Piano parts are written on grand staves (2 staffs), so they often exceed 3 pages. Pianists use a free hand to make necessary page turns.

- **Multi-bar rests:** Sibelius® will ordinarily consolidate rests. In rare instances where it doesn't, check the score to see that there is no conflict causing the part to show one-bar rests. Once you fix the score, the parts will be correct.

- **Odd phrase lengths** (anything other than 4 bars): If you can legibly squeeze 5, 6, or 7 bars onto a line, do it. If not, make each line legible, and make sure the next letter appears in the left margin.

- **Repeats:** Avoid spreading repeated sections past the end of a page.

- **1st and 2nd Endings:** This will often require an odd number of bars per line. If at all possible, don't let an ending continue onto the next line. Make sure the next letter is in the left margin.

Let's apply these guidelines to the **REED 1** part. We will show you where the breaks are, and explain our reasoning (see *Figure 3.5*).

1. Make **A1–5** into a **system** by highlighting those bars and typing **Shift+Alt+M** (⇧⌥M). This assigns the repeated intro to the first system on the page, and places the **Segno** and **Letter A** at the beginning of the second system. It also divides the 10 bars of Letter **A** evenly between systems **2** and **3**.

2. Make **A6–10** into a system. This will put the change of key and Letter **B** at the beginning of system **4**.

3. Letter **B** has 11 bars, so make **B1–5** into a system. This will put the first ending at the beginning of the next system, and leave enough room to place both endings in that system.

4. Make **B6–11** into a system. Letter **C** will automatically have 4 bars, and there will be 4 bars in the next 2 systems.

5. You want to put only 7–8 systems on a title (first) page, 9 if necessary. 10 systems won't usually fit. Even on later pages, 10 systems would probably be too close together for easy reading.

   Select **systems 1–7** and type shortcut **Ctrl+Alt+Shift+M** (⌘⌥⇧M) to **Make Into Page**. That will include **Intro bar 1** through **C8**. In this chart, where page turns aren't a concern (for the reeds and brass anyway), it looks best to keep sections together, so we have opted for only 7 systems on page 1. That keeps all of Letter **D** together on page 2.

(continued p. 56)

REED 1
Piccolo
Alto Sax
Flute

IN A PERSIAN MARKET

Albert Ketelbey
arranged by David Berger

Figure 3.5a: Corrected REED 1 part, page 1.

Figure 3.5b: Corrected REED 1 part, page 2.

6. **D1–4** is already done, so make **D5–9** into a system, **Shift+Alt+M** (⇧⌥M). This puts Letter E at the beginning of the next system—and the rest of the chart is practically done.

7. To make the **Coda** stand out for easy reading, put a gap between this system and the previous one by highlighting one of the bars in the last system and dragging it slightly down the page.

8. To indent the **Coda**, select the final barline of letter **F**, then type **Alt+S** (⌥S), which *splits off* the last system and indents it.

Optimizing Staff Spacing and Reset Note Spacing

After formatting all the system breaks and page breaks for a part, optimize the staff spacing and reset the note spacing.

NOTE: Versions from 2020.1 on have an **Auto Optimize** feature that you can choose to keep on or off.

In the **Ribbon** select **Layout**, under the word **Optimize**, click on **Auto** to toggle it on or off. If it appears in yellow, it is ON.

As with any automatic function, it may not always give the results you want; further adjustment may be needed. The optimizing shown below may not be necessary with **Auto Optimize**—but still, be sure to follow **Steps 1–2** to **Reset Note Spacing**.

1. **Click 3 times** with your mouse on the first bar of the part to **select all bars**.

2. Type **Ctrl+Shift+N** (⌘⇧N) to **Reset Note Spacing**. This will reset any changes that have been made to the default settings in the **Note Spacing Rule** menu. You will notice that a few crammed spots will re-space nicely.

3. With everything still selected, type **Ctrl+Alt+S** (⌘⌥S) to **Optimize Staff Spacing**. This will equalize space between the staves, making

the page easier to read. On simpler parts like **REED 1** of *In A Persian Market*, this won't change much—but you should still get into the habit of optimizing every part.

Workaround to Fix the *D.S. al Coda*

F7–10 should appear as a 4-bar rest, but, because there is a *D.S. al Coda* in bar **F10**, Sibelius® wants to split it into 3 bars and 1 bar. Use this workaround to fix it:

1. Select the *D.S. al Coda* and type **Ctrl+Shift+H** (⌘⇧H) to *hide it* in *just* the **REED 1** part. This will change **F7–10** to a 4-bar multi-bar rest.

2. Make bars **F5–10** into a system, **Shift+Alt+M** (⇧⌥M).

3. Now, go back to the **score view** for **F**. Copy the *D.S. al Coda* and paste it to bar **F6**.

4. Type shortcut **Ctrl+]** (⌘]) to *hide* this in the *score*. It will now show up in all the parts, but *not* the score.

5. Go back to the **REED 1** part. You will now see *D.S. al Coda* above **bar F6**. Select and drag it to the end of **bar F7–10**.

   NOTE: To avoid doing this workaround several times, you need to find a nearby bar in the **score view** with at least one note in it, that will also be on the same page in the **parts view**—hopefully, a bar used by as many instruments as possible. **F6** will work great for all the reeds and brass.

Manual Bar Spacing Adjustments

This is the final step of the formatting process. Go back through the entire part and find any bars that have awkward spacing. Make the appropriate changes, so it looks presentable.

1. Drag the left barline of **Intro bar 8** to the right to make the 7-bar rest and 1 bar of notes look more in proportion to the rest of the chart.

2. Drag the double bar at the end of the 4-bar rest in Letter **F** to the right, until the first two bars of music look more in proportion. (Make sure you drag the barline and not the handle.) After you do this, reposition the *D.S. al Coda.*

3. On the **Coda**, drag the last barline to the right until **bar 1** of the Coda looks in proportion.

4. Do the workaround on p. 43 to move the **repeat symbol** behind the **5/4** time signature in the **Coda**.

Manual System Adjustments

When you optimize the staves, you may notice that the **Coda** is reset—you may need to repeat **Step 7** from p. 56.

Positioning Rehearsal Marks

Type shortcut **Ctrl+Alt+P** (**⌘⌥P**), then press **Enter** (**Return**) a few times, until you see the menu that allows you to close. Then select **Close** to close the pop-up window. Although this plug-in works nearly every time, check to see that each letter is in line with the beginning of each system, and manually move any letters that aren't. Any letters that are not in the margin (such as **G**) should be centered over a barline. After doing this, quickly glance at all of the rehearsal marks to make sure there are no vertical collisions.

Hiding and Showing Text

There are a few text occurrences in the **score** that differ from the **parts**, and vice versa. Learn what these are and how to fix them.

1. In the **score**, we put the name of the instrument for **REED 1** (**Piccolo**) above the first bar of the score. This is so the conductor knows what instrument everyone should be playing. How to make that show *only in the score* was discussed on p. 27.

2. In the **parts**, put the **instrument name** over the first bar of music that each instrument

plays. In the **REED 1** part, create text (**Ctrl+T**) (**⌘T**) over bar **B8**: Piccolo.

3. Select the **Piccolo** text over **bar 8**, then type **Ctrl+]** (**⌘]**) which will make it show *only in the part*. Repeat this for the **REED 2** (**Clarinet**) and **3** (**Bass Clarinet**) instrument text.

Final Steps

1. The slurs in **A10**, **B5–6**, **D9**, and **E8** should be raised manually to avoid collisions and awkward spacing.

2. The **Title** should be raised a bit: Select the title, then press the ↑ arrow about 8 times.

3. Raise the **composer credit** by selecting it and pressing the ↑ arrow 4 times.

When finishing a part, look for these placement issues:

- Text
- Dynamics
- Signs (segno and coda)
- Copyright notice
- Slurs and ties (specifically those that go over system breaks and repeat barlines)
- Rehearsal letters.

The **REED 1** part is ready to print (see *Figure 3.6b and 3.7b*).

Copying the Part Layout

1. Press **'** to open the **Copy Parts Layout** menu.

2. Select **Source part**: Reed 1 will already be highlighted since it was the last part worked on.

3. Select **Destination parts**: Select REED 2, then hold down **Shift** and select **Drums**.

4. Press **OK** on the screen or **Enter** (**Return**) on the keyboard.

5. A pop-up dialog box will ask: Are you sure you want to copy the layout? Select **Yes**.

Extracting the REED 2 Part

Press the plus sign **+** in the upper right corner of your workspace and select **REED 2**. By copying the **REED 1** format, you have reduced the amount of work needed to format the **REED 2** part.

The layouts for some or all of the parts will be identical or nearly identical, depending on how the piece is orchestrated. You will still need to make a few corrections, though (see *Figures 3.7a–b* and *3.8a–b*).

1. Because of crowding caused by the 16th notes at Letter **A**, you will need to redistribute those bars. So, instead of **5** bars per system, use **3**, **3**, and **4**.

2. You will also need to redistribute the number of systems per page. Put **7** systems on page 1, and the remaining **8** systems on page 2.

3. There are two *D.S. al Coda*'s in bar **F7–10**. Click on the lower one, and press **Ctrl+Shift+H** (⌘⇧**H**) to hide it.

4. Triple-click **bar 1**, then Reset Note Spacing: **Ctrl+Shift+N** (⌘⇧**N**).

5. With all the measures still selected, Optimize Staff Spacing: **Ctrl+Alt+S** (⌘⌥**S**).

6. Pull the **Coda** down, as you did in **REED 1**.

7. Select the final barline of **F**, then type **Alt+S** (⌥**S**) to split the **Coda** from the other systems and indent it.

8. Make bars **F5–10** into a system by selecting them and pressing **Shift+Alt+M** (⇧⌥**M**).

9. Look for instances where barlines need to be adjusted. There are two in this part: fix the **Introduction** and **Coda** as in **REED 1**.

Extracting the REED 3 Part

Press the plus sign **+** in the upper right corner of your workspace and select **REED 3**. As you can see, this part's layout is identical to **REED 1**. This is a big time saver. Skip **steps 1–3** from

Extracting the REED 2 Part, and go straight to steps **4–9** (see *Figure 3.8*).

Extracting the Trumpet Part

Press the plus sign **+** in the upper right corner of your workspace and select **Trumpet**. As with **REED 1**, you'll need to determine the formatting of each system.

Text Alignment

The magnetic layout has pushed the **Tempo text:** *Solos – Tpt/Tnr/Pno, Bkds on cue under tpt solo* away from its original position. To manually change its position:

1. Select the text.

2. Hold down **Ctrl** (⌘) and press the ↑ arrow until the text sits properly above the **Tempo text:** *Swing*.

3. Do the same thing at Letter **G** with the **Technique text:** *Harmon Solo – Tacet 1st x* and *Vamp to Fade*.

4. Repeat **steps 4–9** from **Extracting the REED 2 Part** (see *Figure 3.9*).

Extracting the Trombone Part

Open the **Trombone** part and scan it to see if the layout works or needs adjustment. In this case the format matches the **REED 1** part nicely, so skip **steps 1–3** from **Extracting the REED 2 Part**, and go straight to **steps 4–9**.

Like the reeds, the **Trumpet** and **Trombone** parts usually have a similar structure. So, once you edit the **Trumpet**, you can use it to format the **Trombone** part (see *Figure 3.10*), by copying the part layout as you did with Reed 1.

Extracting the Piano Part

The **Piano** part formats differently from the horns, since it uses a grand staff (two staves). Here are a few general rules:

- No more than **5** systems on the first page.
- No more than **6** systems on subsequent pages.
- Dynamics go in the middle, when both hands have written music.
- Dynamics go under the bass clef when playing chord changes.
- No repeat bars in the first bar of a new system! When using chord symbols, each line must start with a chord symbol.
- Don't be too concerned about page turns. When necessary, keyboard players will briefly rest one hand while they turn the page. Classical pianists usually have a page turner for performances.

Because the **Piano** part has a grand staff, the number of systems per page in the **REED 1** layout will not work. To *unlock* the **Piano** part from that format: **Click 3 times** in the first bar of the part and then type: **Ctrl+Shift+U** (⌘⇧**U**).

1. Make **A5–A10** into a system.

2. Because there are notes several ledger lines below the staff, limit this page to 4 systems, and put a page break at Letter **B**.

3. At Letter **B** make systems of 5 and 6 bars.

4. Make **D5–9** into a system.

5. Put a page break at Letter **E**.

6. Make **F1–5** into a system.

7. Make **F6–10** into a system.

8. Triple-click in **bar 1**, then Reset Note Spacing: **Ctrl+Shift+N** (⌘⇧**N**).

9. With all measures still selected, Optimize Staff Spacing: **Ctrl+Alt+S** (⌘⌥**S**).

10. Pull the Coda down, then split it off and indent it, as in the **REED 1** part.

11. Select the final barline of **F**. then type **Alt+S** (⌥**S**) to indent the **Coda**.

12. Around **F7–10** there are two *D.S. al Coda*'s. Select the first and *hide* it by typing **Ctrl+Shift+H** (⌘⇧**H**) (see *Figures 3.11a–c*).

Formatting the Bass Part

Open the **Bass** part. This part is practically done.

1. Make **A1–5** into a system.

2. Make **A6–10** into a system.

3. Make a page break before **C5**. (This will put **C5** through the **Coda** on the same page).

4. Repeat **steps 8–12** from the **Piano** part. (See *Figure 3.12*.)

Formatting the Drum Part

Open the **Drum** part. When we have a lot of repeats in the **Drum** part, we often squeeze 8 or even 12 bars into one system. This will ultimately reduce the number of pages, which is helpful for the drummer, since s/he rarely has rests and needs both hands to play—making page turns awkward. We try to limit **Drum** parts to 2 or 3 pages if possible.

1. Make **bars 1–4** into a system.

2. Make **bars 5–8** into a system.

3. Make **A1–4** into a system.

4. Make **A5–7** into a system.

5. Make **A8–10** into a system.

6. At **B1**, raise the word *Rhumba* using the ↑ arrow. Also fix the collision with rehearsal letter at **E** by selecting the word *Rhumba*, then moving it to the right with the → arrow.

7. Make **C1–8** into a system.

8. Make **D1–9** into a system.

9. Make **E1–8** into a system.

10. Select the *D.S. al Coda* connected to **F6** and press **Ctrl+Shift+H** (⌘⇧**H**).

11. Make **F1–6** into a system.

12. Select the final barline of **F10**. Type **Alt+S** (⌥**S**) to split the **Coda**, then indent it.

13. Repeat **steps 8–12** from the **Piano** part.

(continued p. 73)

6/4/2021

Figure 3.6a: REED 2 part, page 1, formatting taken from REED 1. Needs correction.

REED 2
Clarinet
Tenor Sax

IN A PERSIAN MARKET

Albert Ketelbey
arranged by David Berger

Figure 3.6b: Corrected REED 2 part, page 1.

Reed 2   2   In A Persian Market

Figure 3.7a: REED 2 part, page 2. Needs correction.

Reed 2   2   In A Persian Market

Figure 3.7b: Corrected REED 2 part, page 2.

REED 3
Bass Clarinet
Bari Sax

IN A PERSIAN MARKET

Albert Ketelbey
arranged by David Berger

Figure 3.8: Corrected REED 3 part, page 1.

TRUMPET

Figure 3.9: Corrected Trumpet part, page 1.

TROMBONE

IN A PERSIAN MARKET

Albert Ketelbey
arranged by David Berger

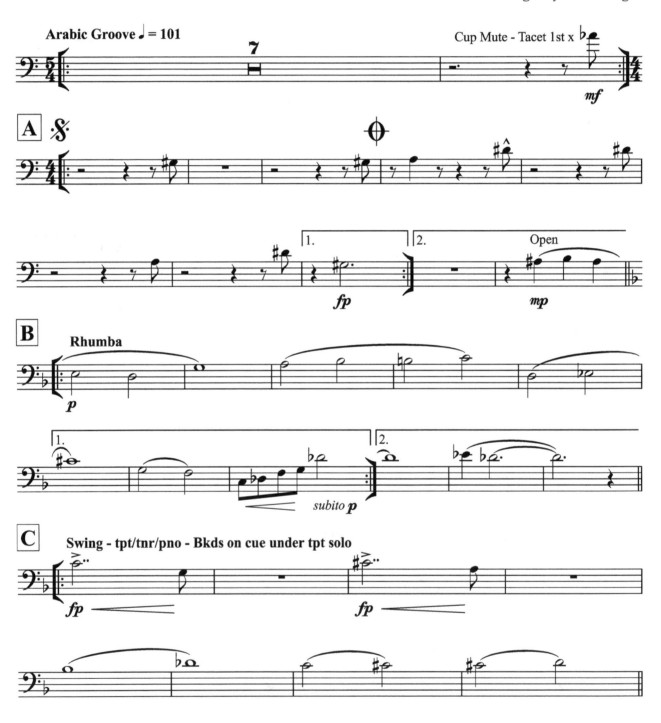

Figure 3.10: Corrected Trombone part, page 1.

PIANO

IN A PERSIAN MARKET

Albert Ketelbey
arranged by David Berger

Figure 3.11a: Corrected Piano part, page 1.

Piano   2   In A Persian Market

Figure 3.11b: Corrected Piano part, page 2.

Piano 3 In A Persian Market

Figure 3.11c: Corrected Piano part, page 3.

BASS

IN A PERSIAN MARKET

Albert Ketelbey
arranged by David Berger

Figure 3.12: Corrected Bass part, page 1.

DRUMS

Figure 3.13a: Corrected Drum part, page 1.

Figure 3.13b: Corrected Drum part, page 2.

Resolving Differences between the Score and Parts

Never put a **repeat bar** symbol (✗) in the **first bar** of a line or page. (You *never* want to make musicians look at the previous line or page to find out what to play.) Correcting this may require you to hide some information in the score or parts.

1. At **B6** in the **Drum** part, select the **repeat bar** symbol.

2. Press **Ctrl+[** (⌘**[**) to make this *only appear in the score*. The **repeat bar symbol** will disappear from the part.

3. Deselect (**ESC**).

4. On the **keypad**, select **Voice 2**.

5. Input 4 quarter notes at **B6**, on the third line of the staff.

6. Holding down **Ctrl** (⌘), click on each note with the mouse, until all 4 are highlighted.

7. Type **Shift**+**Alt**+**3** (⇧⌥**3**) to turn these quarter notes into slashes.

8. With the 4 notes still highlighted, type **Ctrl+]** (⌘**]**). This will make them appear *only* in the **Drum** part.

9. Go back to the score view, and double-check that everything looks as it should.

Notating the Number of Repeats

To make the drummer's job easier, when there are more than three repeat symbols in a row, place the **total number of bars** (the original bar plus the number of repeat bars), centered over the last repeated bar.

1. At **B5** in the **Drum** part, select the final repeat symbol, press **Ctrl+T** (⌘**T**) then type in the total number of bars, centering it over the repeat bar sign.

2. With this text still highlighted, type **Ctrl+]** (⌘**]**) to hide this number in the score. It will now show up in the **Drum** part, but not in the *score;* it's information that a conductor doesn't need to be concerned with.

3. Do this also for bars **C8**, **D7**, **E8**, and **F6** (see *Figures 3.13a–b*).

NOTE: This is used for:
- chord symbols in all instruments
- repeated bars in all rhythm section instruments.

Final Proof

Now that the **parts** are finished, make sure you haven't altered anything in the **score**. Proofread the score twice. The first time, check for obvious problems by giving each page a quick glance. First Proof: Look for major problems such as:

- Random floating text in the middle of a page.

- Accidental transposition of an instrument. (It's possible to hit one key and unwittingly put an entire sax part into the concert key).

- Anything else that immediately catches your eye.

Second Proof: Look for fine details. Spending a few minutes on each page is crucial.

Proofing the Parts

Proof each part individually. This is the music musicians will be reading. They will judge your composition based on these parts. If their focus is distracted by a weird stray bar that stretches an entire system, you will lose their confidence. Think about how you feel when you find misspelled words or bad grammar in a book. When you're sure that everything looks good:

Export the Score and Parts to PDFs

Exporting the Score

About 99 percent of the time, you will be exporting to PDF. Let's start with the score:

1. Select the **File** tab; go to **Export**.

2. Select **PDF** and in the menu, pick **Score Only**.

3. Create a filename. We highly recommend this format for your filenames: **Title SCORE**.

4. Choose a folder to save to. Click **Export**.

    For example, this is how we would name and save our files:
    Filename: **In A Persian Market SCORE.pdf**
    Folder destination: **My Documents > PDF Music > Scores > In A Persian Market**

Exporting Parts

1. Select the **File** tab; go to **Export**.

2. Select **PDF** and in the menu, pick **All Parts Only (one file)**.

3. Create a filename. We highly recommend this format for your filenames: **Title PARTS**.

4. Choose a folder to save to. Click **Export**.

    For example, this is how we would name and save our files:
    Filename: **In A Persian Market PARTS.pdf**
    Folder destination: **My Documents > PDF Music > Scores > In A Persian Market**

Proof the PDF

Our last step in the process is to do a final proof of the exported PDF files. **Never assume that a pdf has exported perfectly.** Anytime you change anything or export a file, proof your work. This proof does not have to be as detailed as the previous proofs—just quickly make sure that you have exported all the right files, and that there are no obvious mistakes.

Lesson 3 Shortcuts Quick Reference			
Ctrl+Shift+Alt+M (⌘⇧⌥M)	Make selected bars into a **page.***	**Ctrl+Shift+U** (⌘⇧U)	**Unlock format** of the current part when whole part is selected.
Shift+Alt+M (⇧⌥M)	Make selected bars into a **system.**	**Ctrl+Alt+Shift+O** (⌘⌥⇧O)	**Open Selected Parts** plug-in.*
Alt+S (⌥S)	Split system into bars or indent Coda.*	**'** (apostrophe)	Open **Copy Parts Layout** menu.*
Ctrl+Shift+H (⌘⇧H)	**Hide** selected object or text **only** in the current part.	**Ctrl+Tab** (⌘Tab)	Toggle from **part to part** or **score to part/part to score.**

* Not standard with Sibelius®. To install, see pp. 6–9.

Finishing Touches

Printing

For **scores** we generally print in black & white, double-sided, on regular **8.5 x 11** inch computer paper. This is standard letter size in the U.S. Most countries in Europe and Asia use a slightly larger size paper, **A4** (297 x 210 mm).

In general, select **Landscape** with **8 bars per page** for ensembles with 20 lines or less. When you select **Double Sided Printing**, click on **Flip on Short Edge**. Select **Portrait** with **4 bars per page** for more than 20 lines. Here, select **Flip on Long Edge**.

Our score template is for an 11 x 17 inch page, so you will need to **Scale** the print to **65%**, or select **Fit To Page**.

For conductors, we print double-sided on special **11 x 17** inch smooth 70 lb. natural or off-white text paper. (White paper would reflect too much light and cause eyestrain after awhile.) Scores are printed with the binding location on the left side.

For **parts**, we use 100 lb. smooth soft white paper specially cut to **9.5 x 12.5** inches. This is the standard size for professional jazz and commercial music in the U.S. Other countries use different size paper. The paper is heavy because it has to stand up to years, possibly decades, of wear.

This size is not commercially available, so we buy it in bulk from a paper supplier and sell the extra reams to other arrangers and copyists.

If you'd like to buy our paper, let us know: visit **www.SuchSweetThunderMusic.com** and click on **Contact Us**.

The part template is set up for an 8.5 x 11 inch page. To print a 9.5 x 12.5 inch part, you will need to **Scale** the print to **114%**, or select **Fit to Page**.

For most commercial work, it is common to print parts on one side and tape the extra pages. It's rare to print double-sided, except for publishing. Players prefer to open a 2 or 3-page part on their stand, rather than have to make a page turn. For long pieces and shows, printing double-sided can be a good option.

Taping

If parts are more than one page, it is essential to tape the pages together. If the pages are separate, players will have difficulty finding all of them, keeping them on the stand, and turning them.

Use masking tape to join pages in accordion folds. Artists' paper tape is the best, but can be expensive. We generally use 3M .5 inch masking tape with a smooth (not paper) finish. Although this tape will not last as long as the artist's tape, it will generally last for 10–30 years, depending on wear and tear.

There are taping machines that attach to a table and do a wonderful job; or you can develop your hand/eye coordination and tape by hand:

Fig. 4.1 Taping a part.

1. Place a piece of cardboard on the table. Cardboard creates enough friction to keep the pages in place while you tape. The cardboard will also protect the surface of your table from razor damage.

2. Place page 1 face up on the left side of the cardboard.

3. Place page 2 face up on the right side of the cardboard, leaving just a hint of daylight between the two pages, and making sure that the tops and bottoms of the pages line up.

4. Grab the edge of the tape in one hand, pull the roll with your other hand until the separated tape is the length of your page.

5. Hold the edge of the tape over the top of the pages, making sure to center it.

6. Hold the other end of the tape (just above the roll) over the bottom of the page, centering it. Make sure the tape is taut; no wrinkles.

7. In one movement, lower the tape to the paper, taking care not to move the paper in the process. It's okay if the top of the tape doesn't quite reach the top of the page.

8. Hold the edge of a razor blade to the tape, lining up the bottom of the page, and pull the roll upward toward your face. This will cut the tape without moving the blade.

9. Use the side of the blade to smooth out and press down the tape from the bottom of the page to the top.

10. If the tape at the top of the page exceeds the page, hold the blade to the edge of the page and draw the blade across the top of the page. This will leave the excess tape to be thrown away.

11. To tape page 3, turn pages 1 and 2 over, so that their blank side is facing up. Page 1 should be on the left and page 2 on the right.

12. Center the outer edge of page 2 on the cardboard. Place page 3 to the right of it, blank side up. Repeat **steps 4–10**.

Continue doing this for any additional pages. Note how we alternate taping the music side up and the blank side up. Accordion folding keeps the sticky part of the tape away from catching other pages, when the parts are folded. Another trick to reduce stickiness is to sprinkle talcum powder in the seams.

Books

It saves rehearsal time to put all the players' parts on their music stands before the start of a rehearsal or performance. We use pressboard folders with the name of each instrument in the upper right corner. It is customary to print the name of the band, orchestra or singer centered in the middle of the page. Since reed players and percussionists (and sometimes keyboardists) play various instruments, rather than label their part **Alto Sax 1**, we call it **Reed 1**. Some bands name this reed part **W.W. 1**, **Wind 1**, or **Woodwind 1**.

Fig. 4.2 A book may need to hold more than 100 pages.

Tacet Sheets

Every player in the ensemble should have a part for each piece and each individual movement of longer works. If certain players do not play for an entire piece or movement, they get a *tacet sheet,* so that they will:

- know their part isn't missing, and
- be able to keep their place in the show.

To create a tacet sheet, use the **header** with Title, Instrument Name, Arranger and Number. This information is common to everyone in the orchestra. The rest of the page should be blank, with the exception of the word: TACET printed in big bold letters in the center of the page.

Sibelius® will automatically create a tacet sheet for each part that doesn't have any notes.

Numbering

We generally number each title, and place each piece in numerical order, to make it easy for the players to find them. Numbers are written in pencil in the upper right corner of the first page of each chart. Make sure that the numbers are large enough to grab the players' attention. But use pencil just in case you might, at some point, want to change the number. This goes along with our general rule to use pencil when writing on parts—**NEVER USE INK**.

The copyists and/or librarians are responsible for putting each book in numerical order for the first rehearsal or performance. After that, it is each player's responsibility to keep his/her book in order. It's also a courtesy to the next person who might play that book.

Shows and Symphonies

When organizing the music for a show with a set order, we number the charts in the order of the show, starting with **1**.

When we start to rehearse shows, there are generally numerous changes. Numbers are added, deleted and moved around; hence we use pencils for numbering. Each chart stands alone.

Once a show is frozen, it is customary to organize the score and parts so that they can be read like a book. They are printed double-sided, and bound. This makes them easier to perform. In each part, make sure to allow enough time for page turns, taking into account the instrument, the tempo, and how many bars of rest will be needed.

The above holds true for lengthy pieces, both symphonic and chamber.

When parts are in books and/or printed double-sided, we **do not use repeats** involving more than **one page, DS,** or **DC.** Those things would be extremely difficult for the conductor and players to do.

Editing

Before computer copying, all changes to the music were written in pencil, or patched in. Players commonly had to decipher road maps with all kinds of directions.

Since editing is so easy in Sibelius®, we usually incorporate changes into the original Sibelius® file, create new PDFs, and print new scores and parts. This makes the players' job much easier. It takes a few minutes and costs money to print, but we highly recommend it. Remember, the goal of music copying is to make the music as easy as possible to understand and perform.

Shortcuts

We highly recommend printing out these pages, and keeping them near your computer as a handy reference.

PC (MAC)	Command	PC (MAC)	Command
Ctrl+↓ (⌘↓)	Move note **down one octave**.	**+** on the numpad	Go to **next Keypad Panel**.
Ctrl+↑ (⌘↑)	Move note **up one octave**.	**Shift** and **+** sign (**–** sign on Mac, no Shift)	Go back to **first Keypad Panel**.*
Alt+B (⌥B)	Open **Create Bars** menu.	Ctrl+P (⌘P)	Open **Print** menu.
Ctrl+S (⌘S)	**Save.**	Shift+T (⇧T)	Open **Transpose** menu.
Ctrl+Z (⌘Z)	**Undo**—Go back 1 step.	Ctrl+Shift+T (⌘⇧T)	Toggles between **Concert** and **Transposed Score**.
Ctrl+K (⌘K)	Create **Chord Symbol text**.	S	Slur to next note. Over a group of notes, slurs them all.
Alt+K (⌥A)	Select **all highlighted chord symbols**.*	Ctrl+Shift+Alt+I (⌘⇧⌥I)	Open the **Instrument Change** menu.
Ctrl+L (⌘L)	Create **Lyric text**.	Ctrl+Alt+T (⌘⌥T)	Create **Tempo text**.
Alt+L (⌥L)	Select **all highlighted lyrics**.*	Ctrl+3 (⌘3) on the numpad	Create **eighth note** in tempo text.
Ctrl+C (⌘C)	Copy **all selected information**.	Ctrl+4 (⌘4) on the numpad	Create **quarter note** in tempo text.
Ctrl+V (⌘V)	**Paste.**	Ctrl+5 (⌘5) on the numpad	Create **half note** in tempo text.
Ctrl+Shift+Alt+T (⌘⇧⌥T)	Open **Edit Text Style** menu.*	T	Open **Time Signature** menu.
Ctrl+Alt+K (⌘⌥K)	Open **Keypad**.		Create a simultaneous vertical pitch **above** a note in the same staff: Select note and type the number of the **interval** (2,3,4, etc.).
Ctrl+0 (⌘0)	**Fit page on screen.**		Create a simultaneous vertical pitch **below** a note in the same staff: Select note, hold down **Shift** and type the number of the **interval** (2,3,4, etc.).
Q	Open **Change of Clef** menu.	Ctrl+T (⌘T)	Create **Technique text**.

* Not standard with Sibelius®. To install, see pp. 6–9.

(continued)

PC (MAC)	Command	PC (MAC)	Command
Shift+**Alt**+**M** (⇧⌥M)	Make selected measures into a **system**.	**H**	Create a **crescendo** hairpin.
Ctrl+**[** (⌘[)	Show information in **score**, but not in parts.*	**Shift**+**H** (⇧H)	Create a **diminuendo** (decrescendo) hairpin.
Ctrl+**]** (⌘])	Show information in **parts**, but not in score.*	**Ctrl**+**Shift**+**Enter** (⌘⇧Return)	Create a **Special Page Break** at selected barline.
Shift+**Alt**+**1** (⇧⌥1)	Turn a note into **x notehead** (useful for cymbals).	**Ctrl**+**Shift**+**N** (⌘⇧N)	**Reset Note Spacing**.
Ctrl+**Alt**+**5** (⌘⌥5)	Create a **Repeat Bar**.*	**Ctrl**+**Alt**+**S** (⌘⌥S)	**Optimize Staff Spacing**.*
Shift+**Alt**+**4** (⇧⌥4)	Change highlighted note to a **specific rhythmic slash**.	**Ctrl**+**Alt**+**Y** (⌘⌥Y)	Open **Transport** panel.
Shift+**Alt**+**3** (⇧⌥3)	Change highlighted note to a non-specific **stemless slash**.	**Ctrl**+**Shift**+**Alt**+**M** (⌘⇧⌥M)	Make selected measures into a **page**.*
Shift+**Alt** (⇧⌥) plus **any number**	Change a note to one of many types of **noteheads**.**	**Shift**+**Alt**+**M** (⇧⌥M)	Make selected measures into a **system**.
L	Open **Lines** Gallery.	**Ctrl**+**Shift**+**H** (⌘⇧H)	**Hide** selected object or text **only** in the current part.
Ctrl+**Shift**+**I** (⌘⇧I)	Open the **Inspector**.	**Alt**+**S** (⌥S)	**Split** system/measures or indent coda.
Ctrl+**E** (⌘E)	Create **Expression text**.	**Ctrl**+**Shift**+**U** (⇧U)	**Unlock format** of the current part once the entire part has been selected.
Ctrl+**R** (⌘R)	Create **Rehearsal Mark**.	**Ctrl**+**Alt**+**Shift**+**O** (⌘⌥⇧O)	**Open selected parts** plug-in.*
Ctrl+**Alt**+**P** (⌘⌥P)	Open **Position Rehearsal Marks** plug-in.*	**'** (apostrophe)	Open **Copy Parts Layout** menu.*
;	Turn a note into a **grace note**.*	**Ctrl**+**Tab** (⌘Tab)	Scroll from **part to part** or **score to part** when one or more parts is open.
/	Turn a grace note into a **slashed grace note**.*		

* Not standard with Sibelius®. To install, see pp. 6–9.
** See *Sibelius® Reference Guide* for additional information.

Index

Other Books by David Berger

Available at **www.SuchSweetThunderMusic.com/collections/ebooks**

*High School Jazz:
A Director's Guide
to a Better Band*

*Creative Jazz
Composing & Arranging*

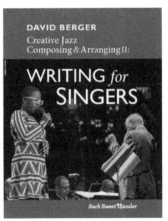

*Creative Jazz
Composing & Arranging II:
Writing for Singers*

*Life in Db
A Jazz Journal*

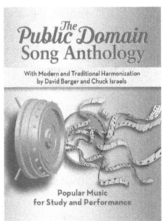

with Chuck Israels
The Public Domain Song Anthology
https://aperio.press/site/books/
series/oer/

About the Authors

Jazz composer, arranger, and conductor **DAVID BERGER** is recognized internationally as a leading authority on the music of Duke Ellington and the Swing Era. Conductor and arranger for the Jazz at Lincoln Center Orchestra from its inception in 1988 through 1994, Berger has transcribed over 750 full scores of classic recordings, including more than 500 works by Duke Ellington and Billy Strayhorn in addition to hundreds of other classic jazz recordings.

In 1996 Berger collaborated with choreographer Donald Byrd to create and tour *Harlem Nutcracker,* a full-length jazz ballet that expands the Tchaikovsky/Ellington/Strayhorn score into an American classic. The 15-piece band assembled to play this show has stayed together as the David Berger Jazz Orchestra. The DBJO actively performs Berger's music on tours throughout the United States and Europe.

Berger has written music for numerous jazz groups of all sizes, symphony orchestras, singers, dancers, television, Broadway shows and films and has served as conductor and musical director for dance companies, TV and stage shows.

Following a career as a trumpet player, Berger served as adjunct professor at a number of jazz studies programs in the New York metropolitan area including The Juilliard School, Manhattan School of Music, The New School, and William Paterson University. He has written dozens of etude books for Charles Colin, as well as jazz composing and arranging books for his own publishing company, Such Sweet Thunder. He writes a weekly blog about the intersection of art and life, which can be found at **www.SuchSweetThunderMusic.com**.

CHRISTIAN DANCY lives in Springfield, Massachusetts, where he works as a composer/arranger, guitarist, music copyist, and educator. Christian holds a BA in music with a concentration in guitar and jazz studies from Westfield State University. He also holds an MFA in Music Composition from Vermont College of Fine Arts.

Christian studied music composition with James Argiro, Andy Jaffe, Michael Early, Diane Moser, and David Berger. His work has been performed locally and across the United States by various rock bands, chamber ensembles, and big bands, as well members of the Bang on a Can All Stars, Jenny Davis Quintet, Spektral String Quartet, and The Boston-based clarinet and marimba ensemble Transient Canvas. Christian's music, regardless of style or ensemble, always focuses on improvisation and the fusion of various musical worlds.

MARC SCHWARTZ is a saxophonist, composer, and arranger pursuing a doctorate in Jazz Studies at the University of Northern Colorado. Marc has played in and arranged for performances in ensembles, festivals, and concert halls around the world. A native of East Northport, New York, Marc earned his BA and Master's degrees in jazz performance and composition at the Eastman School of Music. Afterward, he worked as a musician in New York, where he taught private lessons, performed in venues around the city, arranged for ensembles of all kinds, and formed an octet to showcase his transcriptions and arrangements.

Marc has won 6 Student Awards from *Downbeat* magazine for his arranging, solo saxophone performance and ensemble playing, and was honored by the Jazz Education Network with a 2020 Jamey Aebersold Endowed Scholarship.

He performed as a member of Ryan Truesdell's Gil Evans Project at Prez Fest in New York City and at the 2012 Umbria Summer Jazz Festival in Italy. In 2014, Marc joined the Glenn Miller Orchestra as a tenor saxophonist, performing nationally and in Japan. He also performed on an extended U.S. tour with the national production of *In The Mood*. In 2014, Marc lectured and performed as a guest artist with the Jazz Ensemble at the Escola Profissional de Musica de Espinho in Espinho, Portugal. While pursuing his doctorate, Marc remains in demand as an arranger, orchestrator and music engraver for composers across the U.S.